Body
Sculpting

RACHEL LORKIN

SILVERDALE BOOKS

A QUANTUM BOOK

This edition published by Silverdale Books,
an imprint of Bookmart Ltd., in 2002

Bookmart Ltd.
Desford Road
Enderby
Leicester LE19 4AD

ISBN 1-85605-672-4

QUMBYS

Typeset in Great Britain by
Central Southern Typesetters, Eastbourne
Manufactured in Singapore by Eray Scan Pte Ltd.
Printed in Singapore by Star Standard Industries (Pte) Ltd

In loving memory of George E. Arrowsmith-Lorkin

Dedicated to Pauline, Melanie, Cecille, Edmund, Simon

Warning

All guidelines should be read carefully. If you are pregnant, or
have a medical condition, the exercises in this book should not
be followed without first consulting your doctor. The author and
publisher cannot accept responsibility for injuries or damage
arising from failure to comply with this warning.

CONTENTS

WHAT IS BODY-SCULPTING?

Body-sculpting means redefining our body by using weights to tone, shape, or build up muscle. While it is an excellent way to control our physical shape, it also improves posture, sense of well-being, and boosts confidence. Muscle growth is one of the greatest apprehensions that prevents women from lifting weights. However, there are a variety of weight-training programs available and many different ways to train. The most important issue is to break down the misguided beliefs about shaping your body with weights. Weight-training will not create huge, bulging muscles or a rippled, muscular physique. Such physiques can only be achieved by long hours of dedicated training and complex dieting regimes. This book will be your essential guide on how to train properly with weights so that you can see and feel the benefits for yourself.

The greatest benefit of body-sculpting is that it can be done by anyone, no matter what their fitness level, age or ability. Moreover, the results can usually be felt within a relatively short time. Body-sculpting can be used for gaining muscle strength and has been practised for years by physiotherapists when helping those with severe injuries. Combined with weight-training, body-sculpting will also help strengthen those areas in the body that are prone to injury or weakness, for example, the knee joints and the lower back.

Strengthening and muscle building is usually depicted by the media as a male sport. However, women are now discovering that training with weights has many advantages. Women have often

> *"Body-sculpting means redefining our body by using weights to tone, shape, or build up muscle."*

been dissuaded from training with weights for fear that they will look too masculine as a result. While today there are a greater number of women found in the gym than ever before, there are still many myths surrounding weight-training.

The idea that women should be small, petite, and feminine usually stems from male domination in media and advertising. Fortunately, women are challenging these stereotypes and are entering male-oriented fields in all professions. They are not only breaking myths, but are redefining the way they are perceived. However, there are still some misconceived ideas about women and weight-training, so we need to put the myths behind us and concentrate on the facts.

MYTH ONE

"Training with weights will make you 'muscle-bound' "

It is extremely difficult to become "muscle-bound" to the extent of a man. Men have the hormone testosterone. Women also have this hormone, but in a much smaller quantity. Most women have smaller muscles than the average man, because they have greater quantities of the female hormone, estrogen. Men also have a greater proportion of muscle mass than women, and women carry a slightly higher proportion of body fat to men. So a hugely muscular appearance is difficult for women to achieve no matter how much body-sculpting they do.

MYTH TWO

"Training with weights will reduce your flexibility"

Weight-training involves taking muscles through a complete range of movement. This improves joint and muscle flexibility. A proper workout program will include flexibility training, which involves stretching before and after exercising. This will reduce the risk of possible injury and muscle soreness, as well as increasing the ease with which daily activities are performed.

MYTH THREE

"Training with weights makes your legs bigger"

Muscle growth will push fat already present outward, but a program that includes aerobic conditioning and a nutritionally-balanced diet will contribute to the appearance of shapely legs.

MYTH FOUR

"If you stop training with weights, your muscles will turn to fat"

Nonsense! Muscle and fat are entirely different and it is physiologically impossible for one to turn into the other. What can happen is that when exercise intensity is reduced, or stopped altogether, surplus calories will be stored as fat. If instead you balance your energy intake and energy output, you will not gain weight.

Why use training with weights to stay in shape?

Aerobic conditioning (cardiovascular work) and diet alone are not enough to reshape the body. While aerobic conditioning, such as aerobic classes, is particularly good for burning calories, there comes a time when the calorie-burning efficiency levels out. This is because your body becomes familiar with the routines and vigors of any regular aerobic workout. One way to counteract this levelling off is to vary the type of aerobic conditioning that you do, or to vary the intensity of workouts. It can be difficult to see obvious physical gains in cardiovascular improvement over a short period of time, but the long term benefits can never be underestimated.

Dieting is one way to lose excess pounds and the results can often be seen on the bathroom scale over a relatively short period of time. Quite often, excess pounds can seem to slip away easily, but time after time it becomes more difficult to lose those pounds. The weight then never seems to disappear, no matter how hard you try to diet. Dieting is like a yo-yo, you can lose weight in the short term, only to gain more in the long term.

Dieting is also a very negative way to control your shape. Images of self-deprivation and, more seriously, starvation are conjured up. It is destructive to our happiness, as we don't enjoy depriving ourselves of the food we enjoy. Dieting can also become an obsessive habit and can lead to harmful disorders, such as anorexia nervosa and bulimia nervosa. Furthermore, it does not improve body tone or promote an increase of lean muscle mass. It is the increase in lean muscle tissue that increases our metabolism, i.e. the body's ability to burn energy.

So how does body-sculpting help?

It promotes lean muscle mass

Body-sculpting will increase your lean muscle mass and improve your body's shape and muscle tone. It can be part-specific: that is, you can train those parts of your body that you want to change. Dieting alone does not "spot reduce" fatty areas. However, by combining sensible eating, aerobic conditioning and body-sculpting, you will find that the improvements are significant.

Body-sculpting keeps the aging process at bay

From about the age of about 18, the body slowly begins to degenerate. Muscle tissue begins to decrease, while fatty tissue increases. It is this depletion of muscle and increase in fatty tissue that makes us look older. Training with resistance – body-sculpting – stimulates muscle growth, increasing and promoting lean muscle mass. Therefore, body-sculpting can keep the aging process at bay because we are promoting muscle rejuvenation.

It can accommodate everyone, whatever their ability

Everybody is different and genetics play a vital role in our appearance, our height, the color of our eyes, and how curly our hair is, or isn't. It also determines body type. The old saying – "look at your parents because that's how you'll look in a few years" does ring true. How you look, the type of physique that you have, will all have been determined by your parents. Stop wishing you were taller or shorter – enjoy what you have, by making the most of what you have.

Can you lose body fat by weight training?

The simple answer is "yes." However, we need to overcome the belief that reducing our fat intake will reduce excess body fat. We know that dieting can assist in the reduction of body fat, but dieting can also reduce the amount of lean muscle tissue. This reduction in lean muscle tissue results in a lowering of the body's metabolic rate, and so the physical benefits of dieting alone are short-lived. Dieting often makes us feel tired and lethargic, which is a result of the muscles not receiving the fuel they need to function properly. The body's response to dieting is quite clever. The body's cells don't say, "Hey, no food, let's use all the energy we do have and burn out", instead it says, "No food means we can't do everything, so let's do things really slowly to conserve our strength."

Both muscle and fat cells require energy to perform their tasks. Muscle tissue requires more calories to function; the greater the muscle mass, the greater the metabolic rate. Endurance activities such as running, swimming and aerobics usually result in a loss of body fat rather than promoting lean muscles. However, training with weights will assist in burning calories while it promotes lean muscle tissue development, hence increasing your metabolic rate. The greatest benefit of training with weights is that it can be done by anyone of any age and of any ability, and true gains can be seen. Other positive side effects to be gained are improved posture, greater confidence, a sense of achievement, and the opportunity to meet people with similar interests and goals.

TONING VERSUS BUILDING – HOW DO WE WORK?

o you want to do some weight-training, but you're not sure what goal you wish to pursue. Many programs will focus on your desired type of physique, however you need to consider the time, energy, and dedication that you can put into a training regime;  therefore, you will need to be realistic. If you can only dedicate a couple of hours each week to working-out, you can't expect to look like a bodybuilder. This chapter will focus on what sort of training can be done with weights, and you should be able to understand a little better how the body works, and the benefits of body-sculpting.

So, what's actually involved?

No doubt you will have seen weightlifting during the Olympic Games – well, you could lift weights to become a powerlifter. Or you may have seen Mr. and Ms. Olympia competitions on television, where bodybuilders show their highly-trained physiques. Neither of these types of physiques may appeal to you, but these are two extreme forms of the results achieved by using weights.

Consider that most professional and amateur sports people in all fields – swimmers, tennis players, footballers, cyclists – do some form of weighted workout. Marathon runners may use weights to strengthen their legs. Tennis players may focus on upper body strength to improve the force and speed at which they hit a ball. These athletes do not look overly bulky from carrying too much muscle mass. Similarly, you will not look heavy, bulky or muscular if you do body-sculpting. To create a clearer picture in your mind, read the following glossary of often misunderstood terms.

Weightlifting

This refers to a competitive sport involving very powerful and explosive movements. There are two technical moves, one is called a "clean and jerk" and the other is a "snatch." Olympic lifters train for many years and have a high level of muscle strength.

Powerlifting

Similar to weightlifting, powerlifting involves three competitive lifts: a squat, bench press, and dead lift. (You will come across these exercises in later chapters.) Weightlifters and powerlifters usually have certain genetic characteristics, including short limbs and a high number of what is known as "fast twitch" muscle fibers. Both weightlifting and powerlifting involve working with a heavy weight load, low numbers of repetitions and long recovery periods.

Bodybuilding

Bodybuilding is also a competitive sport in which muscle size and proportion (symmetry) are judged. There is no emphasis placed on body strength, even

though many bodybuilders are extremely strong. A bodybuilding program is very extensive because numerous muscle groups are worked. Because of the training intensity (the number of exercises performed) it takes a great deal of determination, endurance, motivation, and support to become a world-class bodybuilder. Successful bodybuilders have typically low body fat and high tolerance to intensive training over long periods of time. Bodybuilding involves working with a moderate weight load and a high number of repetitions with only short rest periods.

Muscle-conditioning

Competitive athletes use muscle-conditioning to enhance their sporting performance. There are hundreds of muscle-conditioning programs, and body-sculpting could easily be placed under this heading. The aim of body-sculpting is to increase muscle size and reduce body fat; usually it involves performing strengthening, repetitious movements.

Principles of training with weights

The fundamental principle of all weight-training is **overload**. This means that the muscles must be forced to work against a greater load than that to which they are normally accustomed. Muscle size is increased by using a large amount of weights with a low number of repetitions. Body fat may be decreased by using many repetitions with low weight. A well-structured weight-training program should aim to achieve a balance between gains in strength and muscular endurance.

Strength training

By lifting heavy weights with low repetition, strength training is similar to powerlifting or weightlifting, but a greater range of exercises are performed, giving a much broader training program to that of power-lifting or weight-lifting.

Muscular endurance training

For this type of training, you will need to determine the maximum amount of weight that can be lifted at any one time in an exercise. As a starting point, you use half the maximum weight you can lift for

endurance training. You need to complete a minimum of three sets, with 14–16 repetitions for each workout. Once 14–16 repetitions become quite easy to lift with minimal effort, you need to increase the weight, or increase the number of sets performed.

If you are starting a body-sculpting program, it is a good idea to start with light/moderate weights and perform three sets of ten repetitions. You can then concentrate more closely on which muscle group you are using, how it feels when it is being worked, as well as posture and extending the correct lifting technique. Once you have a feel for what you are doing to your body, you can then decide which program you would like to pursue.

Understanding your body and how it works

To understand fitness and the effect that training has on your body, you need to know a little bit about the structure and how your body works. This does not have to be a great deal of knowledge, but an understanding will help you separate fact from fiction. Understanding can help you to know your body's limitations, and can assist you when planning training programs for yourself.

The body is an extremely complex piece of engineering, built up from quite a simple structure – a cell. Cells are the basic building blocks on which the body grows and develops. Within cells, complex biochemical changes occur, which enable us to grow, digest food, move, and create life. Groups of cells combine together to form tissue, organs, and organ systems. The most important systems to the exerciser are the skeletal system, muscular system, and the cardiovascular system.

The skeletal system

The skeletal system consists of approximately 226 bones, and while the reason for having a skeleton may seem ridiculously obvious, the skeletal system is much more than a "bunch of old bones." The bones provide a supportive framework for the body. They protect delicate organs, assist the body's movement, and produce red blood cells. Bones are living organs that change as we grow older. One of the greatest concerns for women today is the bone degenerating

disease osteoporosis. This disease is caused by a loss of calcium and the inability of the bone cells to form new bone. Bone density then degenerates, which means that the bones become brittle and fragile, causing them to fracture under very little stress. Studies now show that women who do some form of weight-bearing activity (e.g. walking, jogging, aerobics) can reduce the risk of getting this disease, or reduce the effects of osteoporosis, if it is diagnosed early enough.

Joints

These are the point at which two or more bones meet, where movement often occurs. The joints we are most concerned with in body-sculpting are the knee, elbow, hip and shoulder. Knee and elbow are hinge joints, while the shoulder and hip are ball and socket joints. A hinge joint does not allow a great deal of lateral movement (side to side), and is usually involved in flexion (making a joint angle smaller), and extension (making a joint angle longer). Ball-and-socket joints, by contrast, allow for greater mobility by allowing lateral movement to occur.

The muscular system

There are more than 600 muscles in the body, most of which are involved in moving the body. Three types of muscle exist: smooth muscle – which lines the arteries and blood vessels; cardiac muscle (heart muscle) and striated muscles, e.g. legs – quadriceps.

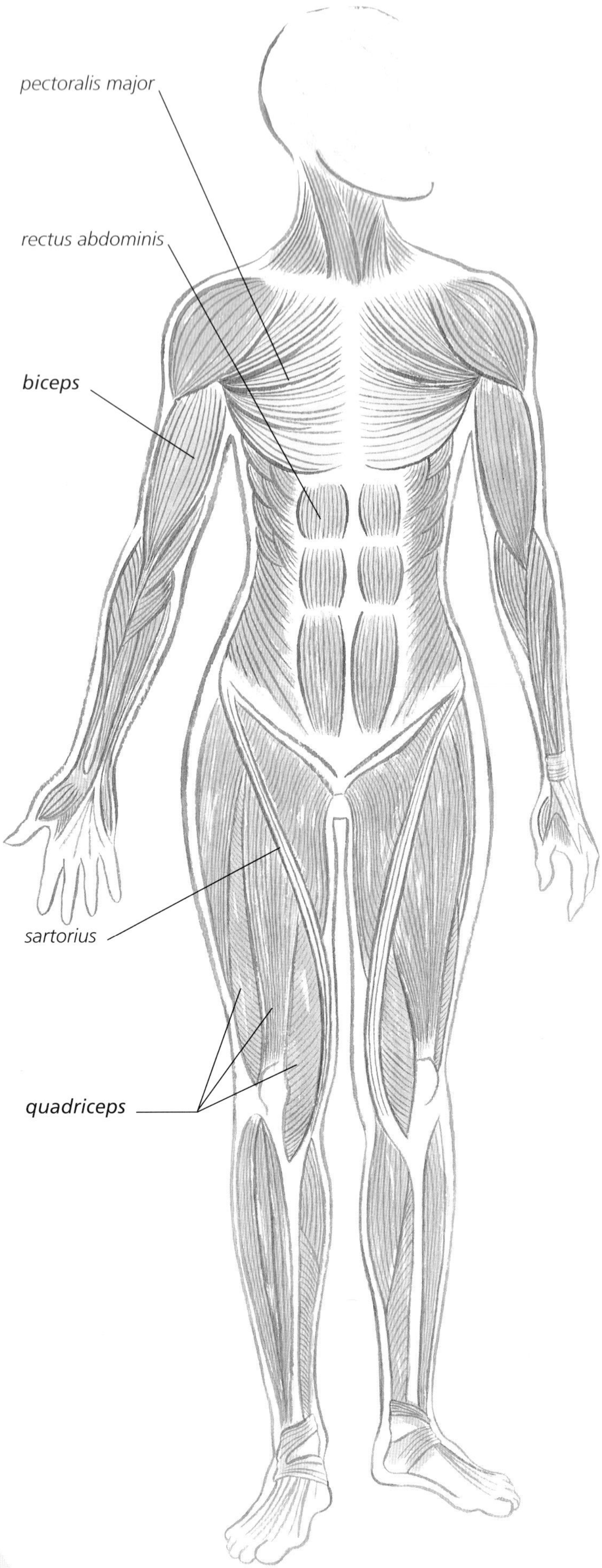

pectoralis major

rectus abdominis

biceps

sartorius

quadriceps

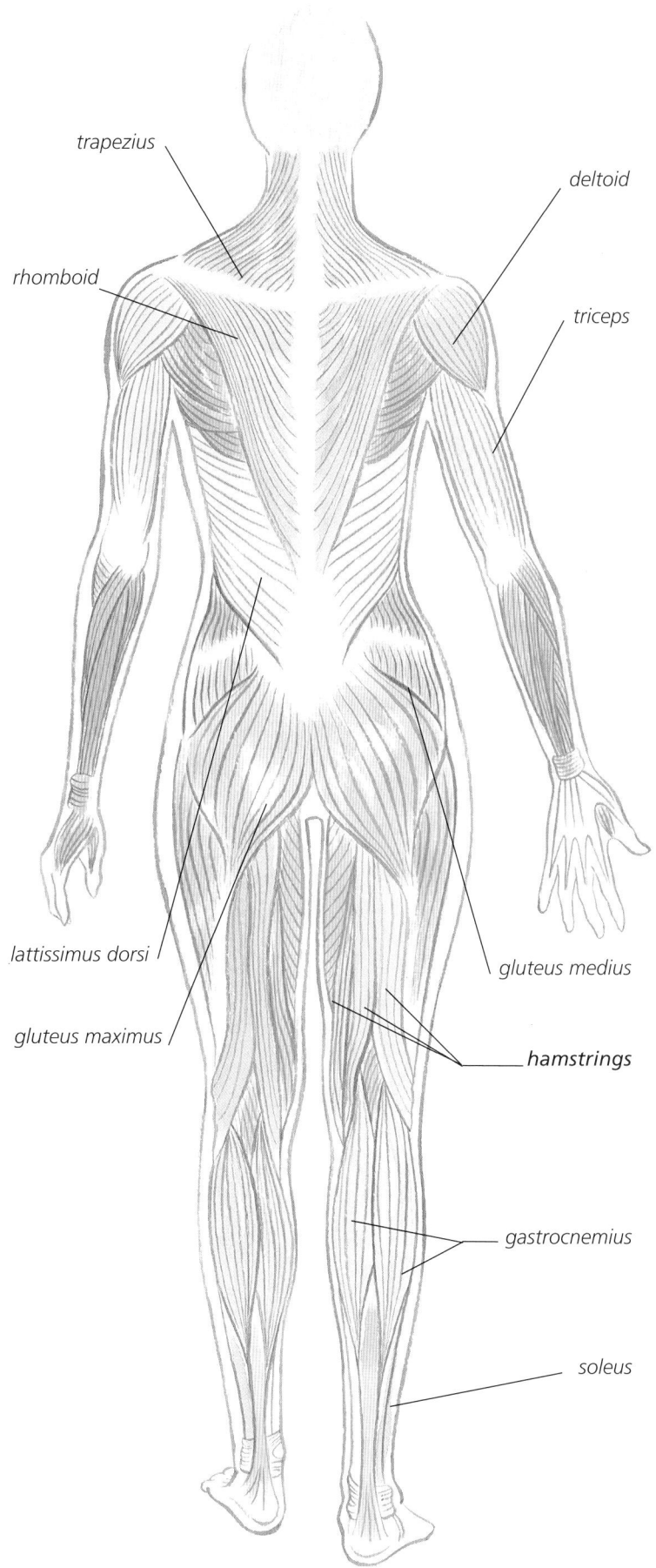

trapezius

deltoid

rhomboid

triceps

lattissimus dorsi

gluteus medius

gluteus maximus

hamstrings

gastrocnemius

soleus

Striated muscles are those muscles used for voluntary movement. Muscles either contract (shorten), or relax (lengthen). To move a bone, one or more muscles (agonist or prime movers), must contract, while others (called antagonists) relax. Effective movement, therefore, requires strength of the prime moving muscle and effective coordination with antagonist muscles. With body-sculpting, we are concerned with skeletal muscle, which makes up approximately 35–44% of our body weight.

Skeletal muscles contain contractile tissues or muscle fiber, which is responsible for contracting the muscle during training. There are two types of muscle fiber: slow twitch and fast twitch. Slow-twitch muscle fibers are slow to fatigue and are used for long-term activities, such as day-to-day activity and long-distance swimming – or running. Fast-twitch muscle fibers are used for quick responses to stimulation, and are prone to rapid fatigue. Therefore, endurance athletes will have built up a greater number of slow-twitch muscle fibers, while powerlifters will have trained to develop more fast-twitch muscle fibers.

Muscles can be contracted in many ways: known as isometric, isotonic and isokinetic. These types of contraction can all play a part in body-sculpting.

Methods for training muscles

Isometric training

With isometric training, no movement of the joint occurs. How does this happen? Energy is needed to create the contraction and calories are burned in maintaining such a contraction. The best example of this is to place the palms of your hands together in front of your chest, and push. You then feel the muscle tighten in the chest, shoulders and upper arm, and there is no actual movement involved in the elbow joint.

This, however, is not an effective way to train as we want to work a muscle through its maximum range of movement. (Isometric training is also believed to have an increased effect on blood pressure.) It is the sort of training where it is beneficial to hold a particular stance for a long period of time. A good example of this is windsurfing.

Isotonic training

Isotonic training means "of equal tension." This means that muscle will develop a tension or force when lifting a load. The force developed by the muscle will be variable, depending on the angle of a joint, and the efficiency of the lever at the joint. An isotonic contraction is one in which muscular force is developed by lifting a constant load through a complete range of movement.

Isokinetic training

Isokinetic contractions require specialized equipment that keeps speed and resistance constant, and promotes muscular development throughout a full range of movement. This allows for the muscle to be overloaded during the whole exercise. This type of equipment is very expensive, so don't be surprised if you don't find it in the local gym.

The cardio-respiratory system

Your body cannot function or survive without oxygen, which is required for all cellular activity. The heart and lungs coordinate the supply of oxygen to the body cells and assist in the removal of waste products. The pulmonary circulation system involves taking deoxygenated blood from the right side of the heart,

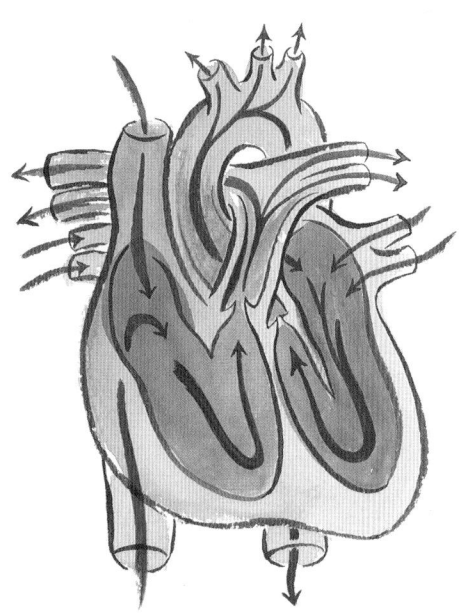

● *oxygenated blood*
● *deoxygenated blood*

via the pulmonary artery, to the lungs for oxygen. Oxygenated blood is then returned to the left side of the heart via the pulmonary veins. This blood is then pumped to the muscles and the body organs.

Exercise increases the cells' demand for oxygen and the need for removal of waste products. It requires the heart to beat faster and the oxygen intake to be greater. If not enough oxygen is getting to the muscles, they become fatigued and usually cease to contract. Vigorous and prolonged exercise thus requires the heart to deliver adequate oxygen to the body with minimal stress. As the heart improves in its ability to deliver oxygen to the body, it will require fewer beats per minute, both during exercise and at rest. Many people confuse a high resting heart rate with metabolism, believing that the higher their heart rate, the higher their metabolism. This is not true. The lower your resting pulse, the better.

To develop a level of aerobic fitness that will enhance the efficiency of the heart, it is necessary to exercise at a rate that pushes the heart rate above its normal capacity. This is usually calculated as 220 beats per minute minus your age, multiplied by 55%. This is the lower end of your range. Now substitute 80% for 55%: this is the maximum rate. It will establish a threshold in which you should work. Here's an example:

Sarah is 35 and has never exercised before:
$$220 - 35 = 185$$
$$185 \times 0.55 = 101$$
$$185 \times 0.80 = 148$$

She needs to initially work at 101 beats per minute and eventually build up, so that her heart rate is at 148 beats per minute.

Heart rate testing can be more individually specific if you use the Karvonen formula which takes into account your resting heart rate.

Sarah's resting heart rate is 75 beats per minute. The formula now looks like this:
$$220 - 35 = 185$$
$$185 - 75 \times 0.55 = 60.5$$
$$185 - 75 \times 0.80 = 88.0$$

Sarah is unfit. The basic formula has over-estimated her effective working level, but the Kanvone formula is more realistic for Sarah's capability.

For effective aerobic benefit of the cardio-respiratory system, you need to train within your training threshold – 55–80% of the maximum heart rate for between 20–40 minutes **at least** three times per week. (As recommended by the American College of Sports Medicine.) If 15 minutes is all you can do – keep it up, you'll get there.

Training methods

The best thing about a body-sculpting program is that individuality can be taken into account. Some people will respond better to certain methods of training than others. The following points will be a guide to the way you can train and overload those muscles!

Pyramiding

This is carried out by increasing the load used, usually set by set, or repetition by repetition, and usually characterized by a decrease in repetitions. For example, you decide that for bench press you will do ten repetitions at 45 lb for the first set, then for the second set you will do eight repetitions at 55 lb, then for the third set, six repetitions at 65 lb.

Reverse pyramiding

Here the load being lifted is decreased as in pyramiding but the number of repetitions are increased for each set.

Forced repetitions

This requires the assistance of a "spotter", who can give assistance at the difficult part of the exercise. This is where the muscle will be weaker, therefore forcing the weight to be moved through its full range of movement.

Super-setting

A method where you combine two movements without a rest between each exercise. This method can be used for the same muscle group, e.g. pectorals, or for opposing muscle groups, e.g. biceps and triceps.

Blitzing

This is the practice of bombarding a particular muscle in a training session with the aim of working the muscle to complete fatigue.

How often should you train?

This is completely up to you and your schedule. If you can manage 30 minutes per time, do some really beneficial work: combine muscle groups and get to it. The following examples suggest when and how to train:

1 Three times per week, e.g. Monday, Wednesday, Friday
   Day 1 – back, biceps
   Day 2 – chest, shoulders, and triceps
   Day 3 – legs
   – always include time for warm-up and abdominal work, and cool down and stretch.

2 Two times per week, e.g. Tuesday and Thursday
   Day 1 – back, biceps, hamstrings, and calves
   Day 2 – chest, triceps, quadriceps, and shoulders

3 Four times per week, e.g. Monday, Tuesday, Thursday, Friday **or** Saturday, Sunday, Tuesday, Wednesday
   Day 1 – back, chest, and quadriceps
   Day 2 – biceps, triceps, and hamstrings
   Day 3 – back, biceps, and shoulders
   Day 4 – chest, triceps, and legs

Training intensity

Training intensity can be increased in three ways:

1 By increasing the load of the weights used; or
2 Increasing the number of repetitions; or
3 Increasing the speed and duration of a workout.

Don't be afraid to challenge your body and experiment with your training. Finding the workout that works well for you can be half the challenge. These points will also help to defeat boredom.

> You must remember that nothing happens overnight: both time and effort will get the desired results. Be positive in the knowledge that you have already started on the road to great physical shape.

GETTING PREPARED

For many people, the image of the gym is one of muscle-bound men and women, looking very serious and intimidating. As with anything new that you pursue, be it a career, hobby or sport, it can take a bit of getting used to, but you usually find

that if you persist, it all makes sense. It is a great way to meet people who all have a common interest – their health. In this chapter you will find guidelines to help select the right gym for you, and information on the type of equipment you will be using. Making use of gym equipment will add variety, efficiency, and comfort to your workout.

Before starting any fitness program you should first of all get your doctor's approval. This is particularly important if you have ever suffered from any long–term illness. You should be able to discuss with your doctor any health-related problems: for example, high blood pressure, diabetes, back or neck problems, arthritis or angina, in addition to the fact that you want to undertake an exercise program. Most doctors will encourage exercise and should be able to discuss the sort of program required to suit your needs.

What do you do next?

Starting any serious body-sculpting or toning program will involve using weights, hence the use of a gymnasium or the purchase of weight-training equipment. Your choice will depend on the size of your wallet. The advantages of using a gym are the range of equipment usually provided, a motivational atmosphere and advice when you need it. Disadvantages can be that it is crowded, noisy (usually with loud music), and expensive.

The advantages of training at home are that you can train to suit your own timetable and you are not paying for any extras that you would not use in a health club, e.g. the sauna. You can also build up your own knowledge and confidence. Disadvantages of training at home are the initial expense of buying equipment, not finding the time to train and losing motivation, as there are no comparisons that you can make between yourself and the way others train. The choice will be a personal one, but please don't fall prey to the "I must be 'in shape' to join in a gym" syndrome.

Here are some guidelines to help you select the right gym for you

● It is wise not to purchase long-term or lifetime memberships on your first visit to the gym. Get a short-term membership and gain a feel for the atmosphere and the type of people using the gym. Some gyms may offer a free number of days' training and, better still, may offer an introductory induction program to prospective clients.

"Begin with a basic weight training program to become proficient at lifting weights."

- If there is more than one gym in your area, visit them all and train in the ones that you feel most comfortable with.

- Is the club clean and safe? Are the staff friendly, helpful and well-trained? Is there too much machinery and not enough free weights? Does the machinery look well-kept and well-maintained? If you are new to the area, is there a place for socializing? Are there crêche facilities?

- If you are starting out, you should request an induction program so that a member of staff can show you how to use the equipment properly and safely. They should be able to design a program that meets your specific requirements.

- Get what you want. Never be afraid to say you want to do serious bodybuilding. Don't be dissuaded or discouraged, be persistent. However, be realistic: while you may want to look like a bodybuilder, if you have never trained with weights in your life, then you will need to start a basic weight training program to become proficient at lifting weights.

The type of equipment you will be using

There is really no mystery to gym machinery and equipment and, like any sport or hobby, once you master the jargon that goes with the territory, "it's a piece of cake."

There are two basic types of equipment, **free weights** and **machines**. You can use either free weights or machines, but a well-balanced program will usually include both. Much speculation has been raised as to which are better at working the muscles and giving shape and definition. Using machines will generally keep the movements more strict and controlled. Free weights, it is believed, allow for a greater range of movement. Working with both free weights and machines can have advantages.

Free weights
Standard free weight equipment consists of **barbells** and **dumbbells**. Barbells may have weights called "plates" added to the end, which are secured with

collars. Most gyms will have racks of barbells with pre-determined weights so that you do not have to load and unload plates.

Most gyms will have what is known as "Olympic bars", roughly weighing 45 lb. These are used on what are called "Olympic benches" for bench press, squat racks and deadlifts.

At first, Olympic bars themselves may be too heavy to lift, so work your way up to using them. It is often easier to use an Olympic bar with one to two plates, than a barbell with five to ten plates at each end. Dumbbells are the mini version of a barbell. They are available in pre-set weights, e.g.from 2½ lbs, 5 lbs, 7 lbs, 10 lbs and up in 5 lb progressions to 80 lbs. The problem for women trainers is the large difference between each progression. For example, going from a 20 lb dumbbell to a 30 lb is demanding. However, some exercises can be performed using plates as an alternative to dumbbells, e.g. for triceps kickbacks. Or some dumbbells can be adjusted so that small plates can be added to increase load.

Machines

Machines come in all sorts of shapes and sizes. In most instances they will have a stack of weights or hydraulic pressure that can be increased or decreased accordingly

The clothing that you will need

Workout gear has become a huge fashion industry, with lycra being the most important workout fashion discovery in the 20th century.

It is not important to wear any special clothing for weight-training. Clothing that allows the body to perform a full range of movement is all that is important.

Athletic shoes

Wear good athletic shoes with a non-slip surface. It is easy to stub toes on equipment that has been left lying around. Feet should be protected in case a weight falls. Never train in bare feet.

Non-essential, but practical items

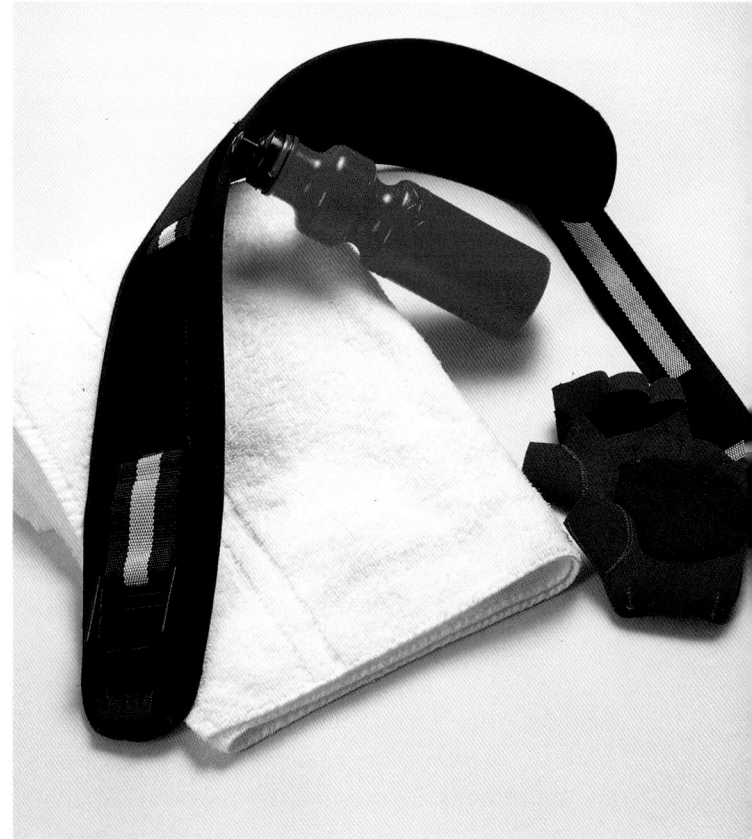

Gloves – not essential for weight-training, but helpful when it comes to gripping bars or machines. They also help prevent callouses from forming on the hands.

Weight belts – useful for supporting the lower back when lifting heavy weights, e.g. for exercises such as squats and dead lifts.

Water bottle – it is important to take a water bottle to the gym. Training hard is thirsty work and you will be saved the expense of buying bottled water.

Towel – having a small towel is often quite handy for wiping down sweaty benches, or using on the benches themselves when training.

Terminology

As with any sport or hobby, body-sculpting has a vocabulary all to itself. You will hear words such as "reps", "sets", and "load." After a short time, these words and their meaning will become second nature, but at first it may seem a little confusing. The following is a list of terms and their general meaning:

Repetitions (reps)

This is the number of times a weight is moved through an entire range of movement in a particular exercise.

Repetition maximum

A technical term for the maximum number of times that the particular exercise can be repeated safely.

Load

This is the weight to be lifted and is usually measured in pounds.

Sets

The number of groups of repetitions in an exercise. For example, "three sets x ten reps bench press" means that there are three groups of ten repetitions of bench press, with a rest period between each set.

Cheating

Carrying out an exercise with another part of the body, which lessens the effect of the exercise on the particular muscle group that is being worked. A good example is the lower back being used to swing the upper body.

Sticking point

The point where further movement through the exercise seems impossible, but with further effort, or the assistance of a "spotter", this can be overcome.

"Spotting"

Where a person assists in the performing of an exercise to overcome the sticking point or to assist when muscle fatigue occurs during the exercise. The person assisting is called a "spotter".

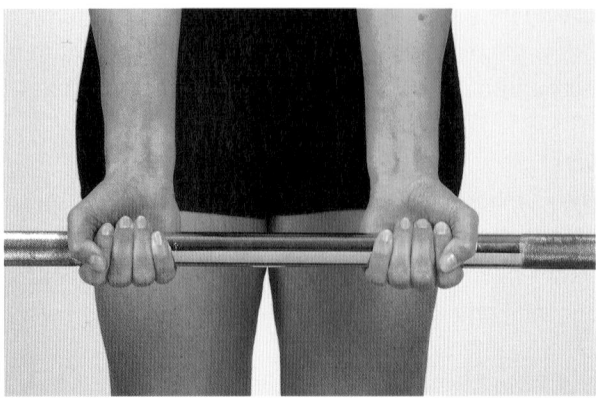

Underhand grip

This is where you grip the bar from underneath the bar; your palms will be facing upward toward the ceiling.

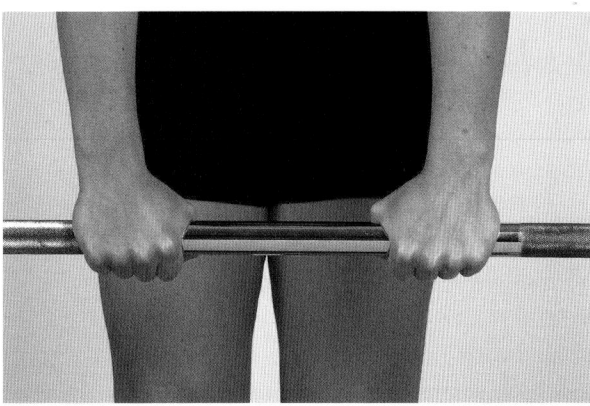

Overhand grip

Where you grip the bar from the top, in this case your palms will be facing downward toward the floor.

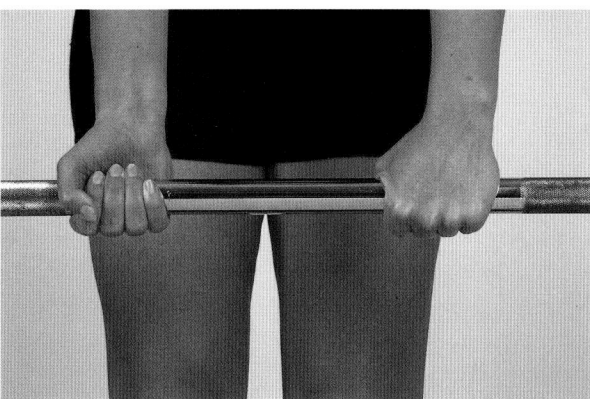

Alternate grip

Simply a combination of the overhand and underhand grip, that is useful when lifting heavy weights.

Throw away the bathroom scale

Do not gauge your body shape by your body weight. The bathroom scale may indicate a change in your body mass, but it will not tell you the ratio of muscle and fat. Remember: muscle tissue is heavy, so it can seem as though you are doing all the right things to lose, yet still gaining weight. Since your goal is body-sculpting, you should be more interested in where you are gaining or losing inches.

Keep a record of your progress

Buy a small notebook or diary and dedicate it to your training. Measure not only your vital statistics (chest, waist, and hips), but the circumference of your calves, lower, middle and upper thighs, forearms and upper arms. Re-measure every six to eight weeks and see how well you are doing.

Be aware of your posture

Be aware of your posture and train with good posture at all times. If you are aware of flaws in your posture, try to correct them. The most common flaw is rounded or slumped shoulders. So check your posture. Are you sitting and standing tall?

Posture also says a lot about a person's confidence. When you walk, do you look at the ground or do you look straight ahead? Watch supermodels on the catwalk and study the way they walk and hold themselves. You don't see too many round shouldered models! Good posture makes you look confident and self-assured – sensuous.

Breathing technique

It is important not to hold your breath when lifting heavy weights. Breathing patterns usually involve breathing in when you work with gravity, and breathing out when you work against gravity. Or, put another way, you should breathe out when you are pushing or lifting weights.

Lifting technique

Lifting barbells, plates or any weight off the floor requires good technique. If you are not careful, much stress can be placed on the lower back, which can result in back injuries.

Tips on correct lifting technique:

- Always bend the knees when lifting weights from the floor
- Make sure your back is "flat" so that the legs are used to lift the weight, rather than the back
- Keep your head up always ensure sure that your body weight is greater than the amount of weight being lifted

WARMING-UP AND STRETCHING

If you have ever watched the Olympic Games, you will notice that no athlete will ever perform their particular event without doing some form of warm-up and stretching exercise. Warming-up and stretching help prepare your entire body for the exercises that follow, and are vital to good performance and injury prevention. The body's internal temperature is increased by warming-up, while stretching increases the range of movement around a particular joint. An added benefit is a healthy massage of internal organs. This chapter will give you ideas on how to warm-up and exercises for stretching the muscles you will be working when body-sculpting.

Warming-up

A warm-up is vital prior to beginning any type of vigorous exercise. It is particularly important for weight-training workouts as muscle strains and soreness can be avoided or minimized. In general, warm-ups usually involve a rhythmic movement of the entire body, the purpose of which is:

- to increase circulation of blood to the muscles
- to gradually increase the body temperature
- to stimulate the heart and lungs
- to prepare mentally for the workout
- to prevent muscle and joint injury

A warm-up should ideally last between eight and twelve minutes. The length of the warm-up may depend on the climate: for example, in cooler climates a warm-up should be a little longer than in, say, a hot climate. If you are warmed up, you should be feeling slightly hot and sweaty!

Warm-up exercises can include:

- Stationary cycling
- Walking briskly, or light jogging on a tread-mill
- Using a rowing machine
- Stairmaster
- Running on the spot

Stretching

Gymnasts and dancers often have incredible flexibility, which they have developed from a very early age. While flexibility is an important component of overall fitness, often little emphasis is placed on stretching because it does not develop muscular strength or burn calories.

Please don't underestimate the power of stretching and its benefits. Many small injuries are caused by the body's inflexibility. Flexibility also decreases as we age: therefore, by stretching regularly, we can keep the aging process at bay and enjoy a better quality of life as we get older.

For body-sculpting purposes, stretching complements the toning and strengthening benefit of training. Muscles lengthen while stretching and, therefore, decrease the risk of potential injury, enabling the full development of opposing muscle groups. Without regular stretching, joints lose flexibility and are unable to move adequately through a full range of movement. It is also a great way to relax and decrease stress levels.

The most effective method of stretching for warming-up and cooling-down is what is known as **static stretching**. This involves the gradual stretching of a muscle and does not involve any sudden or jerking movements. You should aim to coax muscles and joints to mild tension and sustain the stretch. During the warm-up stretch this will be slightly shorter than during the cool-down phase of your workout. Warm-up stretches should be sustained for at least ten seconds and cool-down stretches for up to 30 seconds.

The following stretches are aimed at assisting and preparing the major muscles used in weight-training programs. They can also be performed after any physical workout, in which your body has been put through its paces.

Quadriceps

Standing upright, grip one foot firmly and lift the foot up towards the bottom keeping knees aligned. If you have difficulty balancing, hold gently onto a wall for support only. To increase the stretch, push your foot against the resistance of your hand. This stretch can also be done lying on your stomach or lying on your side.

Hamstrings

This stretch can be done standing, or lying on the back. In a standing position, one foot is placed forward and kept straight, while the supporting leg is bent. The body weight leans forward slightly to take weight off the bent leg.

When standing, you can also use a bench and extend the leg. One foot is rested on the bench with the heel. With a straight back, gently lean forward so that you can feel your hamstring stretch.

Lying on the back to stretch the hamstrings may be more appropriate for the cool-down, where you can relax. One leg will remain bent at the knee, foot planted on the floor close to the buttocks while the other leg is pulled gently toward the chest. The leg may be straight or bent at the knee depending on your general flexibility.

Calves

The standard exercise is a standing calf stretch. You press one leg behind you, with the supporting leg slightly bent. The back heel should be pressed to the floor and your feet should be parallel, rather than turned in to out.

Gluteus (Buttocks)

Lying on the back, bend both knees and place one ankle on the other knee. The supporting leg then lifts toward the chest. You can use the arms, but it is not necessary as the legs are strong enough to push a stretch here. The upper body can stay relaxed while you concentrate on your breathing technique.

Chest

The chest muscles are usually indirectly stretched when stretching the shoulders. This exercise stretches the shoulders, chest, and biceps. Place your hands behind the back and grip together. Move the hands away from the back, keeping your shoulders and head up. This is also an excellent stretch for habitual computer users.

Another stretch starts by placing the palms of your hands onto your lower back, then pushing the elbows back together.

> *"Warming-up and stretching are vital to good performance and injury prevention."*

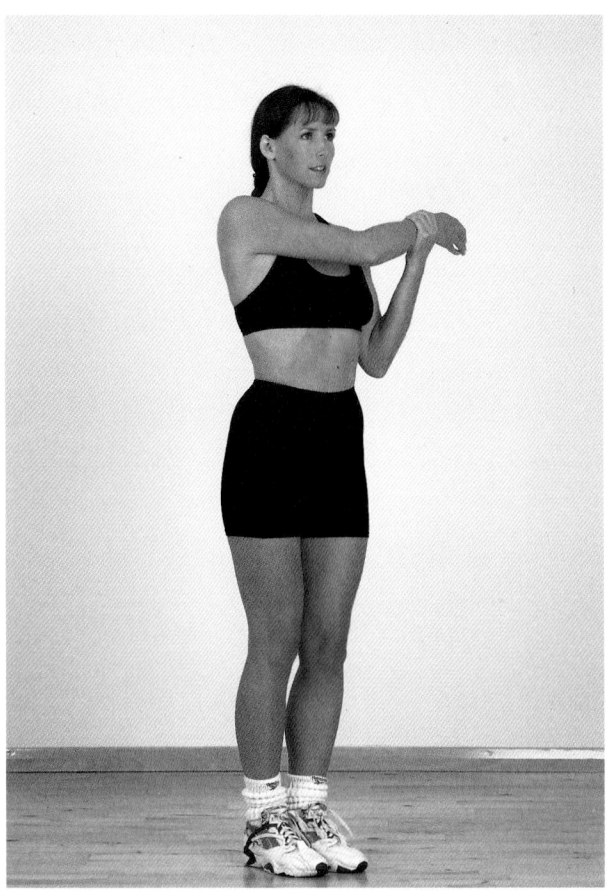

Shoulders

Our shoulders are in constant use and deserve a good stretch (keep this in mind if you work at a desk all day).

Standing shoulder stretch This stretches the posterior muscles in the shoulder and upper back. Standing upright, one arm crosses the upper chest and the other arm gently pulls the elbow toward the shoulder.

Supported shoulder stretch Using a wall, etc. for resistance, stand sideways. Place your hand on the wall, palm facing down. Slightly turn the body to feel a stretch in the anterior shoulder muscles.

Triceps Raise one arm to the ceiling with elbow beside the ear. From the elbow drop the forearm and hand behind the head. With your other hand reach over and gently push the elbow inward toward your head. You can also lean slightly to one side so that you get a stretch into the trunk of your body.

Triceps stretch

Human hands and arms are extremely sensitive and flexible, and are among the most efficient manipulating devices in nature. Having strength in the arms will assist in performing those tasks

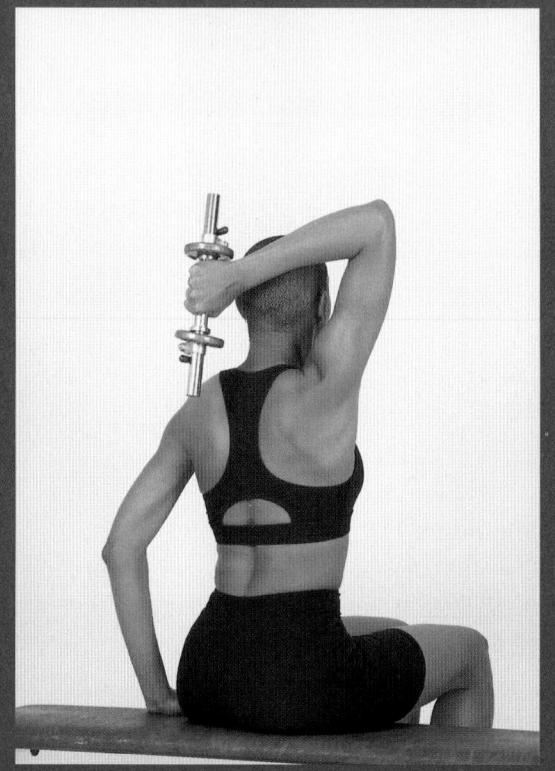

where a little more effort is required, such as lifting and carrying. Women are especially weak in arm strength, with slackness along the back of the arm a common problem. Because that area gets little work it will respond swiftly to toning. The following exercises are designed to improve tone, strength, and shape in the arms.

The arm muscles are grouped into two main areas: the upper arm and lower arm (forearm). The upper arm muscles consist of the biceps and triceps, which control the up and down movement of the forearm.

Biceps

The biceps has two heads (points of attachment to a bone), whereas the triceps has three heads – long, lateral, and medial.

Biceps brachii The biceps is a muscle of the elbow and radius joints, and is primarily associated with flexing and turning the forearm. It has two heads, with both the long and short heads crossing the shoulder joint. It therefore assists in the abduction, or movement, of the shoulder.

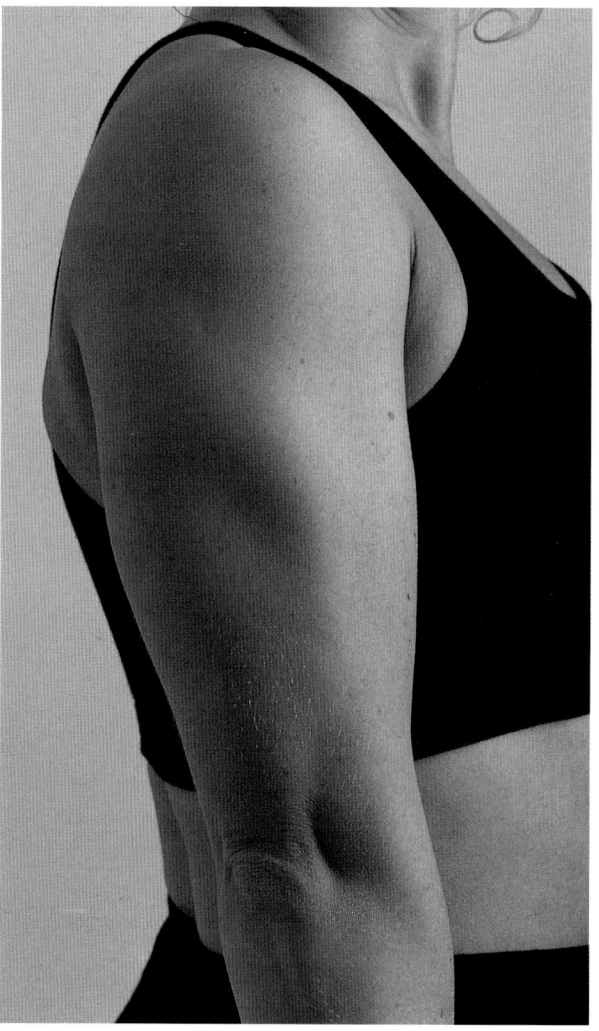

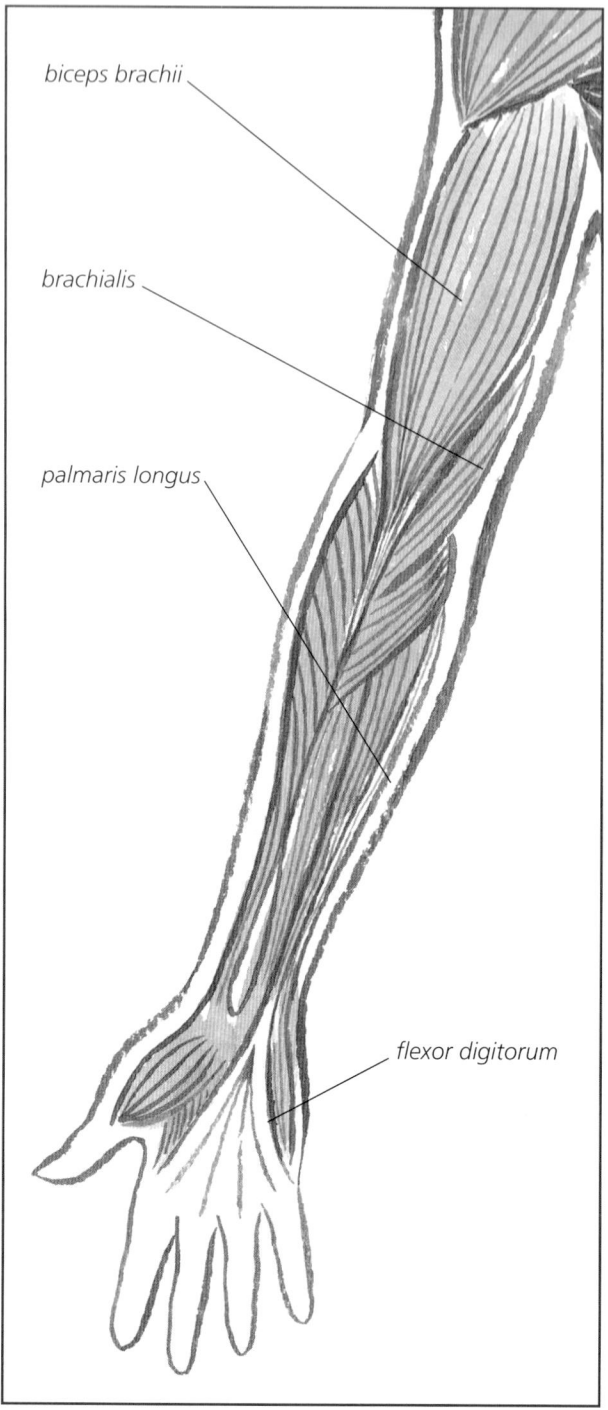

Brachialis This is a deep muscle, which is partially covered by the biceps brachii. Its sole function is flexion of the elbow joint and it is active with the forearm in a prone, supine and semi-prone position.

Brachioradialis This muscle can be found on the anterior upper half of the radius (in the forearm) and it is a contributor to elbow flexion.

STANDING BICEPS CURL

Standing biceps curl

This exercise develops muscles in the biceps and brachialis, as well as the muscles in the forearm.

This is a standard biceps exercise. While standing with the feet shoulder-width apart, knees slightly bent, the arms grip a barbell in an underhand grip. The movement starts from the thighs and the forearms move toward the chest. Keep the back straight and the upper arm just to the side of the body. The weights should be lowered slowly and you should not lean backward.

This exercise can be varied by having a slightly wider or narrower width grip which emphasizes the inner or outer biceps. This exercise can also be performed while sitting.

PREACHER CURL

Preacher curl

This exercise uses the bulk of the lower biceps and brachialis and helps lengthen the muscles of the upperarm. Here the arms are rested over a "preacher" bench with the elbows being fixed. Using an underhand grip, the forearms are flexed toward the shoulders, then lowered slowly.

This exercise can be varied by substituting dumbbells for barbells.

DUMBELL CURL

Dumbbell curl

This routine uses and stretches the biceps but differs from the barbell in that it allows for independent development, where one arm is stronger than the other. It can be performed while standing or sitting and the lift can be performed using both weights together or alternatively. To maximize the contraction, a twist can be added into the exercise at the top of the curl.

REMEMBER

■

Keep your wrists straight

■

Don't let your lower back swing

■

Use controlled movements with appropriate weight

CONCENTRATION CURL

Concentration curl

Use this curl to develop "peaking" of the biceps. This exercise makes use of gravity by moving through a full range of movements. It requires a bent-over seated position, where the elbow is supported on the inside leg near the knee. The forearm moves from the floor toward the shoulder and back to the floor. This creates great stress on the biceps, so keep the movements slow and controlled.

TWO-ARM CABLE CURL

Two-arm cable curl

This movement develops muscles in the biceps and brachialis. The action is identical to a standard biceps curl. However, the tension is maintained through the full, upward movement. This exercise can be varied by using one arm at a time so that unilateral independent biceps strength can be developed.

"Vary your routines to get great shape and tone into your arms."

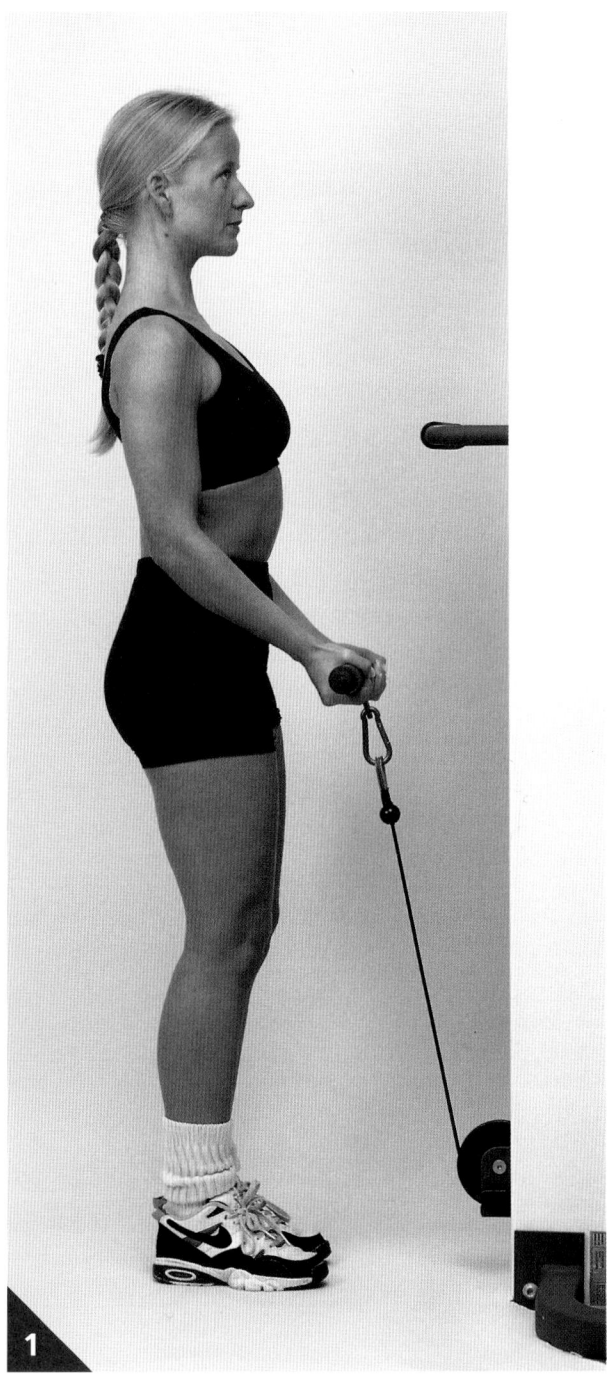

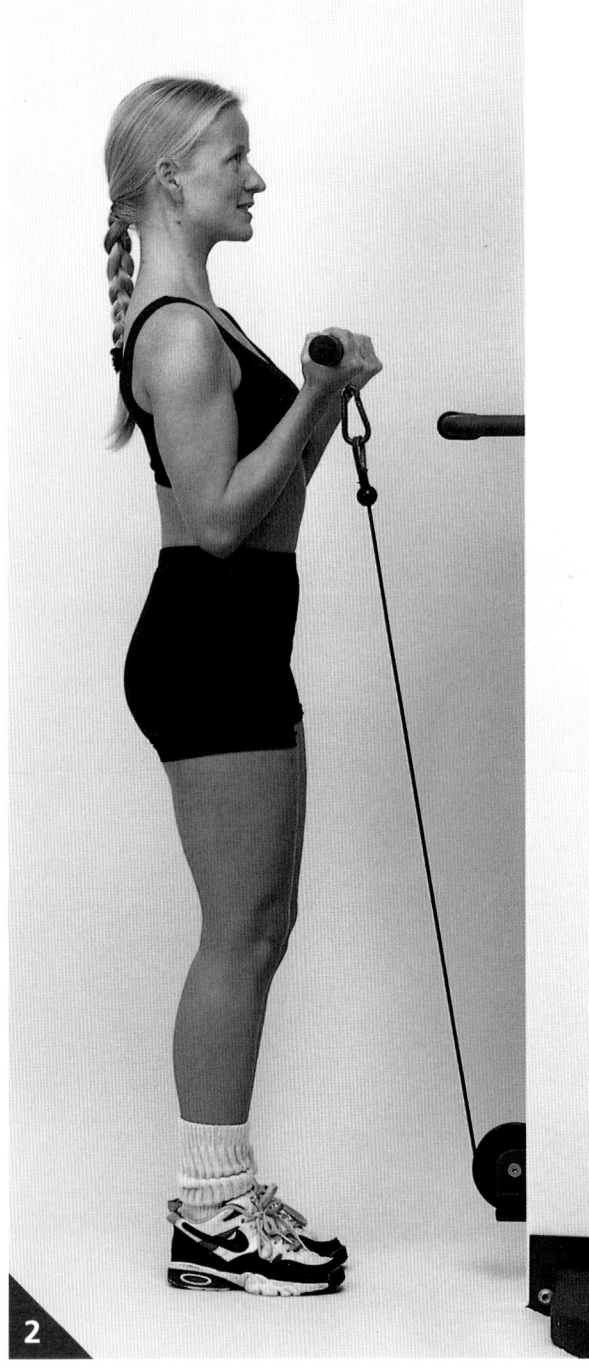

REVERSE GRIP PULL DOWN

Reverse grip pull down

Here the biceps are used in an action involving the latissimus dorsi (the muscles between the ribs and back). This requires using a lat pulldown machine, where the palms are facing the body and the elbows are pulled down toward that body, then extended toward the top of the machine.

WORKOUT ROUTINE 1

Basic biceps workout
Standing or seated dumbbell curls
3 sets x 10 reps
Two-arm cable curls on machine
3 sets x 10 reps
Preacher curls with barbell
3 sets x 10 reps

Strength workout
Standing or seated dumbbell curls
4 sets x 10 x 8 x 6 x 2 reps
Concentration curls
4 sets x 10 x 8 x 6 x 2 reps
Preacher curls with barbell
4 sets x 10 x 8 x 6 x 2 reps

Endurance workout
Standing or seated dumbbell curls
4–5 sets x 14–16 reps
Two-arm cable curls on machine
4–5 sets x 14–16 reps
Preacher curls with barbell
4–5 sets x 14–16 reps
Concentration curls
4–5 sets x 14–16 reps

BARBELL EXTENSION

Triceps

This muscle is found at the back of the upper arm and is responsible for extending both the arm and the forearm. There are three heads to the triceps muscle, "tri" meaning three. These are the triceps long head, medial head and lateral head. All of these are worked in the following exercises:

Barbell extension

This movement can be carried out standing or lying down. For beginners, it may be easier if you lie down.

The bar should be held in an overhand grip, shoulder-width apart, over the chest. Elbows should be kept stationary, and the movement involves dropping the forearms back over the head. The forearms are then raised over the head to the starting position. *Note: If lying on a bench or standing, the back should not be arched.*

This exercise can be varied by having a slightly wider or narrower grip.

> *"Don't be afraid to train the muscles in your arms. Having slight muscle definition is sexy."*

TRICEPS PUSH-DOWN

Triceps push-down using machine

This is an excellent exercise for working on triceps definition as the movement requires working through a greater range of movement. A cable or pull-down machine is necessary for this exercise. It is important to keep the elbows steady and positioned by the body. The weight should not be so great that the arms are pulled forward from the elbow.

Holding the bar shoulder-width apart, the bar is pushed downwards until the arms are straight, then slowly released to the starting position.

REMEMBER
■
Breathe out as you push down
■
Keep your elbows stable
■
Don't stand too far from the cable machine

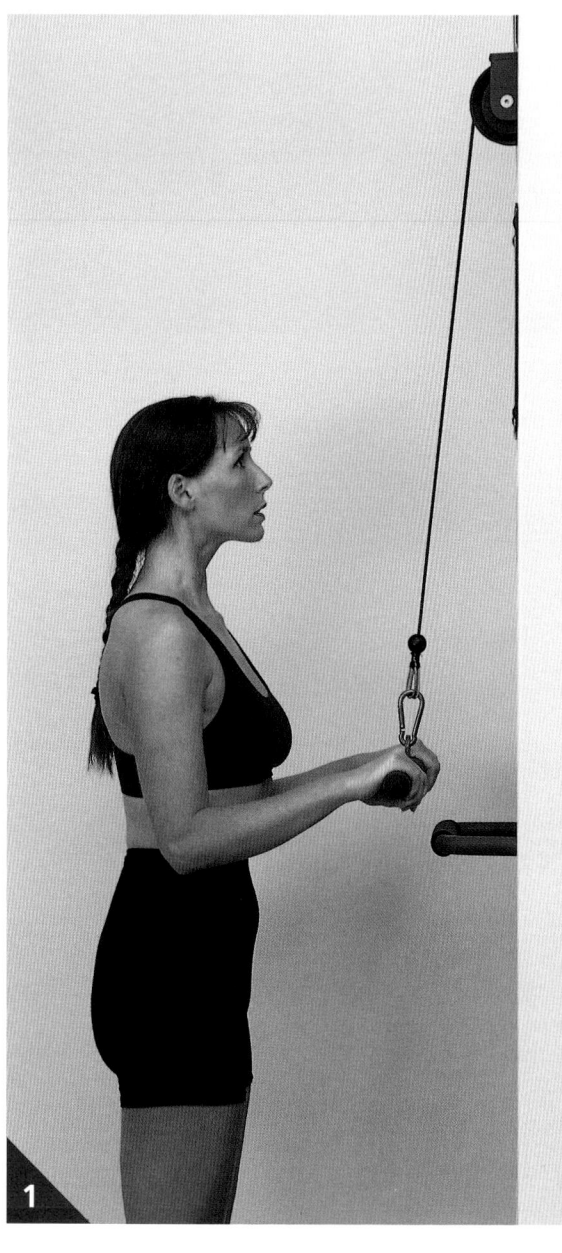

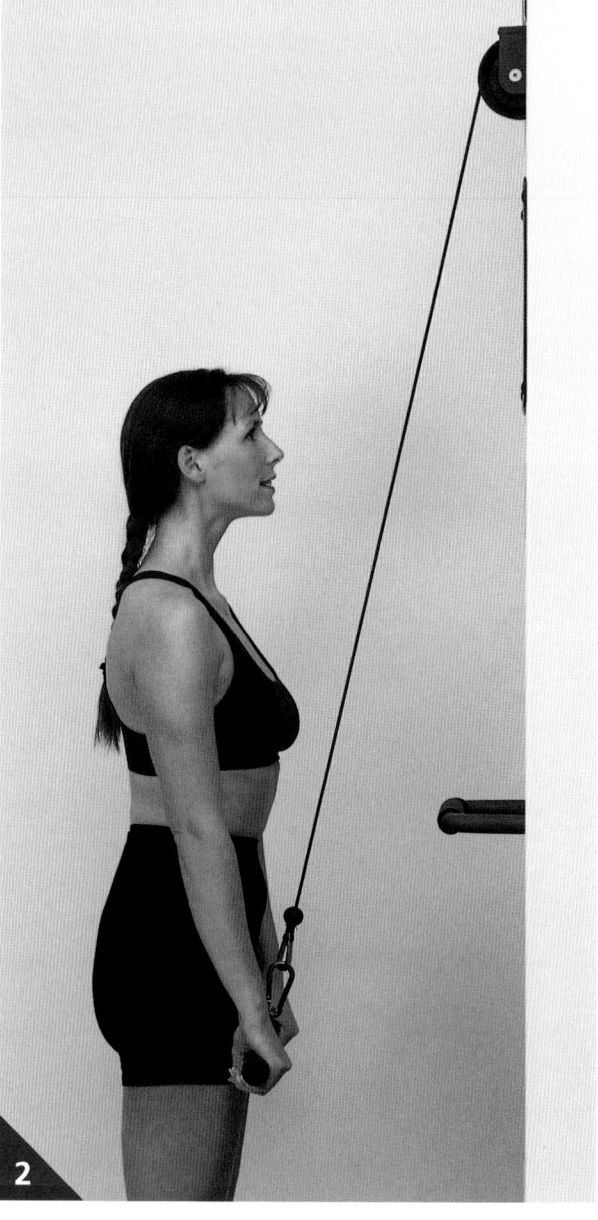

DUMBELL EXTENSION

Dumbbell extension

This exercise can be done in a seated or standing position and is performed one arm at a time. It is great for working the outer triceps, while allowing for a difference in arm strengths.

A move similar to a barbell extension, but instead the palms face inward, which stress the outer triceps. The movement involves holding the dumbbell over the head in an underhand grip. (Note: the elbow will be close to the ear.) The forearm then drops, to behind the head, keeping the upper arm stable. Slowly push the dumbbell back up to the starting position again.

TRICEPS PRESS

Triceps press

The body position needs to be bent forward so support your body weight by holding onto the back of a bench, if possible. Raise the upper arm with the lower arm relaxed, keeping the elbow stable. The forearm pushes upward until the arm is straightened, the forearm is then lowered to the starting position. It is important to keep this movement strict and not let the upper arm move about.

1

2

"Wearing gloves will help to prevent sore hands and callouses forming."

DIPS

Dips

This is an excellent exercise for developing size and strength in the triceps. It also works the back and the chest. It is a hard exercise, but worth it. Try one dip, then next time aim for two, and so on. You can easily get to do three sets of ten reps! Because it is a difficult exercise, it is recommended that you do these dips after warming-up, prior to lifting any weights.

Start in an upright position gripping the bar (palms facing inward). Next, bending from the elbow, lower yourself down toward the floor. Using the arms – triceps – lift yourself up again to the original upright position. It's tough, but you can do it!

WORKOUT ROUTINE 2

Basic triceps workout
Standing triceps push-down on machine
3 sets x 10 reps
Barbell extensions
3 sets x 10 reps
Triceps press
3 sets x 10 reps

Strength workout
Dips
3 sets x 10 reps
Standing triceps push-down on machine
4 sets x 10 x 8 x 6 x 2 reps
Barbell extensions
4 sets x 10 x 8 x 6 x 2 reps
Triceps press
4 sets x 10 x 8 x 6 x 2 reps

Endurance workout
Standing triceps push-down on machine
4–5 sets x 14–16 reps
Barbell extensions
4–5 sets x 14–16 reps
Triceps press
4–5 sets x 14–16 reps
Dumbbell extensions
4–5 sets x 14–16 reps

BARBELL WRIST CURL

Forearms

The forearm has a large number of muscles and tendons involved in moving the hand and fingers. When working the biceps, the brachioradialis will play a significant role in the forearms as it assists in the flexing of the forearm. Other muscles include palmaris longus, which is responsible for flexing the wrist, flexor digitorum superficialis flexes the middle of the fingers, and flexor pollicic longus flexes the thumb.

Keep in mind that forearms are worked extensively during a biceps workout. However, for those looking for a truly serious arm workout, you can include forearms.

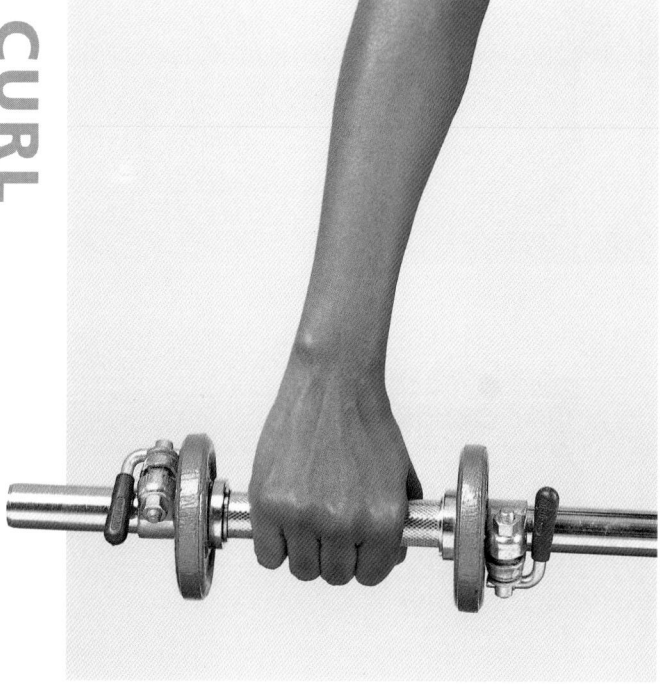

Barbell wrist curl

This exercise strengthens the flexor muscles and is an isolation exercise used for the forearms. The whole arm should remain stable and the elbows can be supported on a bench. Hold the bar in an underhand grip, one shoulder-width apart. The bar is moved toward the body, from the wrists, then lowered back to the starting position.

REVERSE BARBELL CURL

> *"Always keep in mind those myths and remind yourself that training with weights will not make you big, but fat certainly will."*

Reverse barbell curl

This exercise works the forearm and the outerhead of the biceps. The hands are one shoulder-width apart in a grip in which the palms face down. Movement starts at the thighs and the bar is moved up toward the chest by the forearms, keeping the elbows stable. The bar is then lowered to the starting position.

REVERSE BARBELL WRIST CURL

Reverse barbell grip curl

Similar action to barbell wrist curls, however, the grip will be overhand rather than underhand. The movement involves pushing the bar downwards from the wrist, then lifting to the starting position. This is a good exercise for the outside extensor muscles in the forearm and is useful for preventing tennis elbow and over-use syndrome.

WORKOUT ROUTINE 3

Basic forearm workout
Barbell wrist curls
3 sets x 10 reps
Reverse grip barbell curls
3 sets x 10 reps
Reverse barbell curls
3 sets x 10 reps

Strength workout
Barbell wrist curls
4 sets x 10 x 8 x 6 x 2 reps
Reverse grip barbell curls
4 sets x 10 x 8 x 6 x 2 reps
Reverse barbell curls
4 sets x 10 x 8 x 6 x 2 reps

Endurance workout
Barbell wrist curls
4–5 sets x 14–16 reps
Reverse grip barbell curls
4–5 sets x 14–16 reps
Reverse barbell curls
4–5 sets x 14–16 reps

EXERCISES FOR THE SHOULDERS

By using weights we can enhance naturally broad shoulders and a slim waist. Those with narrow shoulders can use weights to create an illusion of being broad shouldered.

By developing the back and shoulders, in addition to trimming excess fat from the waistline, you can create a "V" shape. Toning the shoulder muscles, the deltoids, will not only help ease the strain caused by being hunched over a desk all day, it will significantly improve posture. Whether we lift heavy weights or pick up a leaf, we use muscles in the upper arm and shoulder (deltoids). The exercises in this chapter are aimed at developing the deltoid muscles.

The shoulder

Movement of the arms from the shoulder requires flexibility of muscles, tendons, and ligaments around the shoulder joint. This is the most flexible joint in the body and arm movement includes not only the deltoids but also the upper back muscles, the trapezius and rhomboid.

The deltoid forms a triangle-like cap over the shoulder. The origin of the muscle is the anterior surface of the clavicle and the insertion of the humerus. There are three names associated with the deltoids – anterior, middle, and posterior. These are fibers positioned in location to the joint. The anterior deltoid are responsible for flexing and moving the arm inward. The middle is responsible for abduction of the arm (movement away from the body). The posterior deltoid extends and allows for rotation.

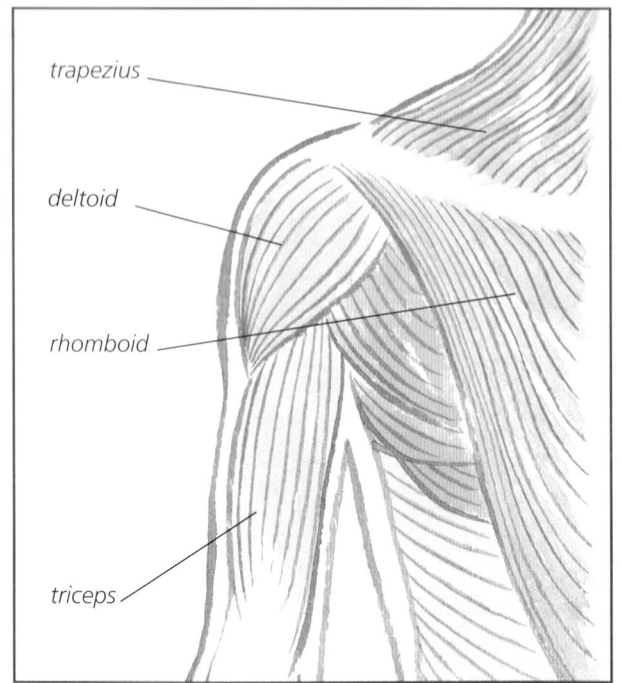

LATERAL RAISE

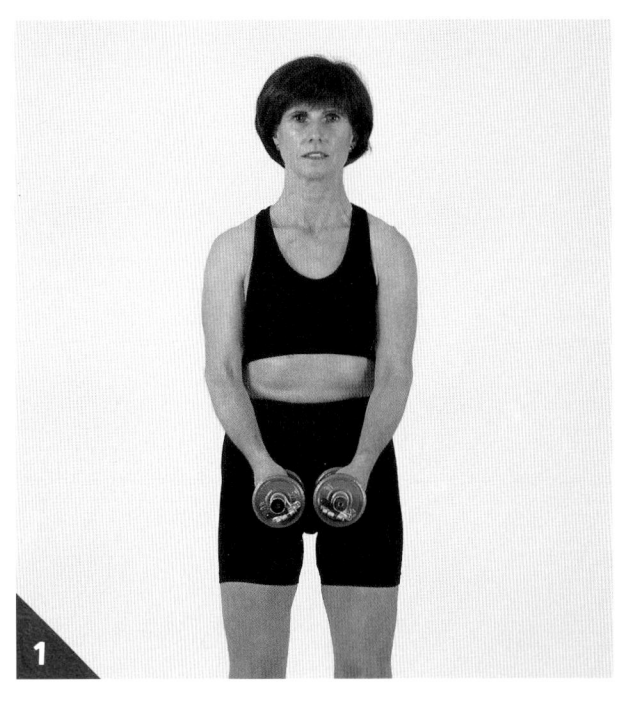

1

Lateral shoulder raise

Using dumbbells, this is an excellent exercise for strengthening and developing the deltoids. With dumbbells in each hand and palms facing downward, the arms start at the thighs and are moved laterally to shoulder height. The elbows should be soft, so as to reduce pressure on the joint. It is also important not to arch the back.

This exercise can be varied by being seated. It is performed in the same manner as the standing lateral raise; however, the movement will be stricter.

2

MILITARY PRESS

Military press

This exercise works the deltoids and the triceps. It places pressure on the lower back, so beginners or those with lower back problems must take great care and start with light weights. Generally performed with a barbell, the military press can be varied using a machine or dumbbells. You can be seated or standing depending on how comfortable you feel while performing the exercise.

The bar grip should be overhand, and the bar should be held slightly wider than the shoulders. The movement involves raising the weight from the front of the chest to a full arm extension over the head without arching the back or locking the elbow joints.

This exercise can be varied by pressing behind the neck, which involves varying the start position from in front of the chest to behind the neck.

It can also be varied by using dumbbells. Start the move with the dumbbells at shoulder height and, from the shoulder, press over the head alternatively using each arm.

"Use the weights to trim and tone the shoulder muscles and significantly improve posture."

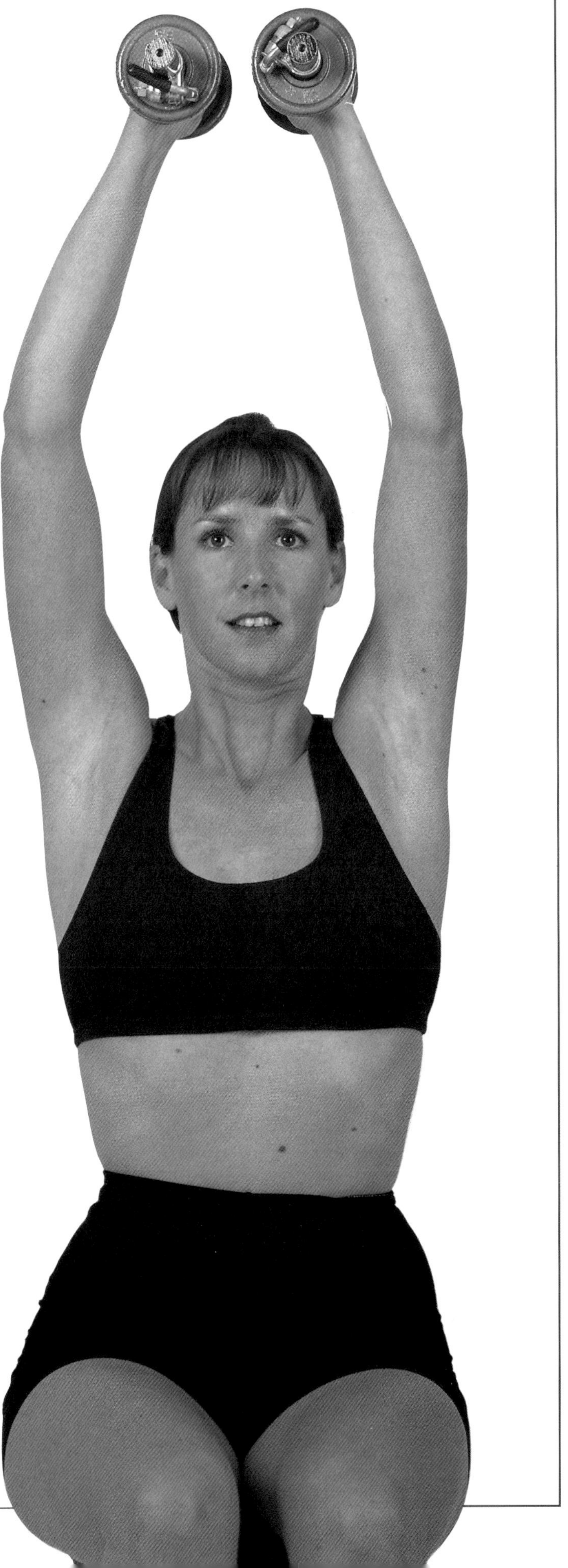

2

1

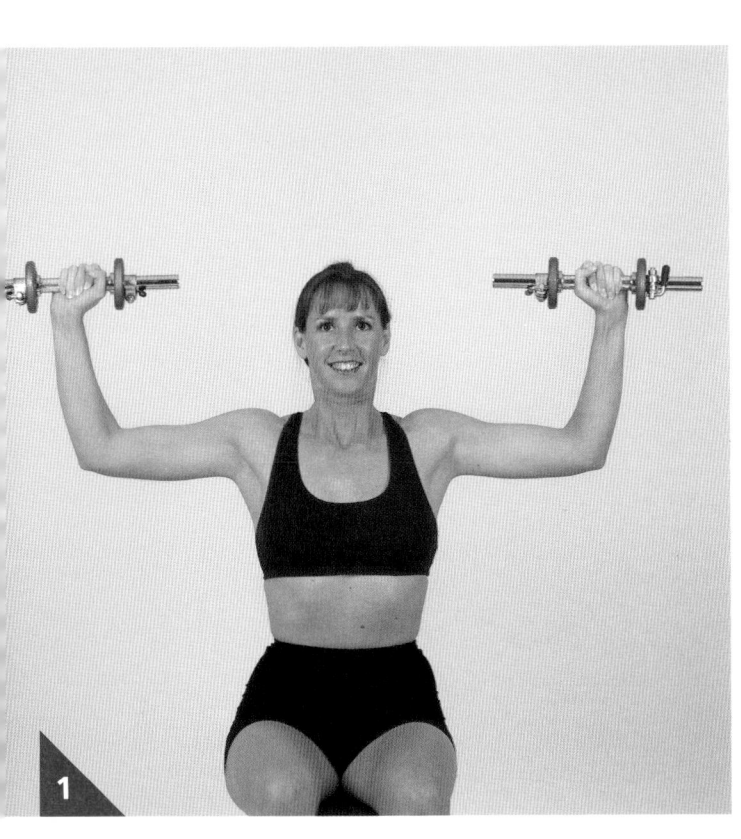

CABLE LATERAL RAISE

Cable lateral raise

A machine with cable pulley can be used, that will provide continuous tension throughout the movement. The action is similar to that of using dumbbells and can be done in a seated or standing position.

Start with the arms extended, holding the bar in an underhand grip no more than one shoulder-width apart. Keep the elbows pressed into the body and move the lower arm up toward the chest, then lower to the starting position. It is important to keep the wrist straight and not to use the forearms or back to pull the weight.

> **REMEMBER**
> ■
> It is important you do not over-stretch the shoulder in this exercise. The deltoids work effectively when the arm is raised to shoulder height.

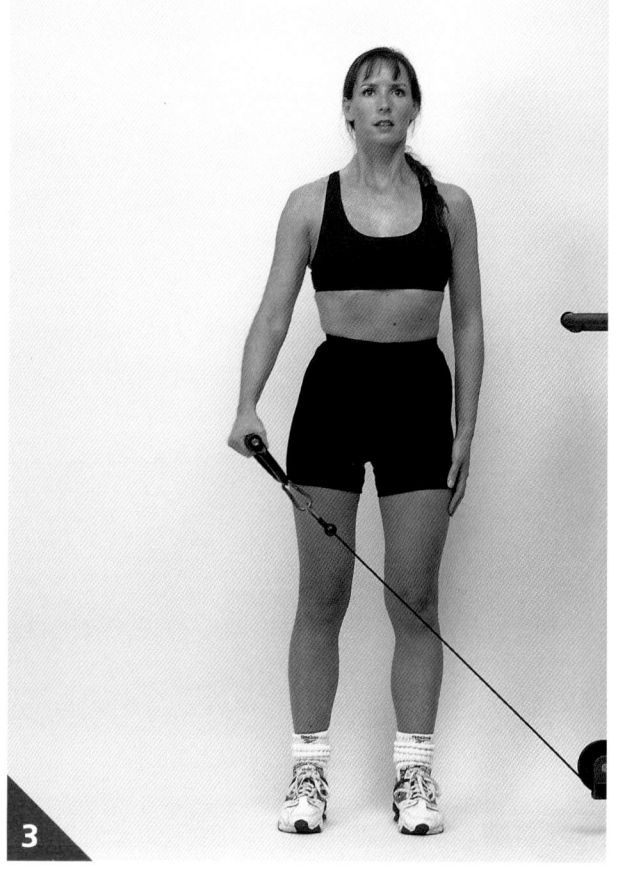

4

CABLE LATERAL RAISE

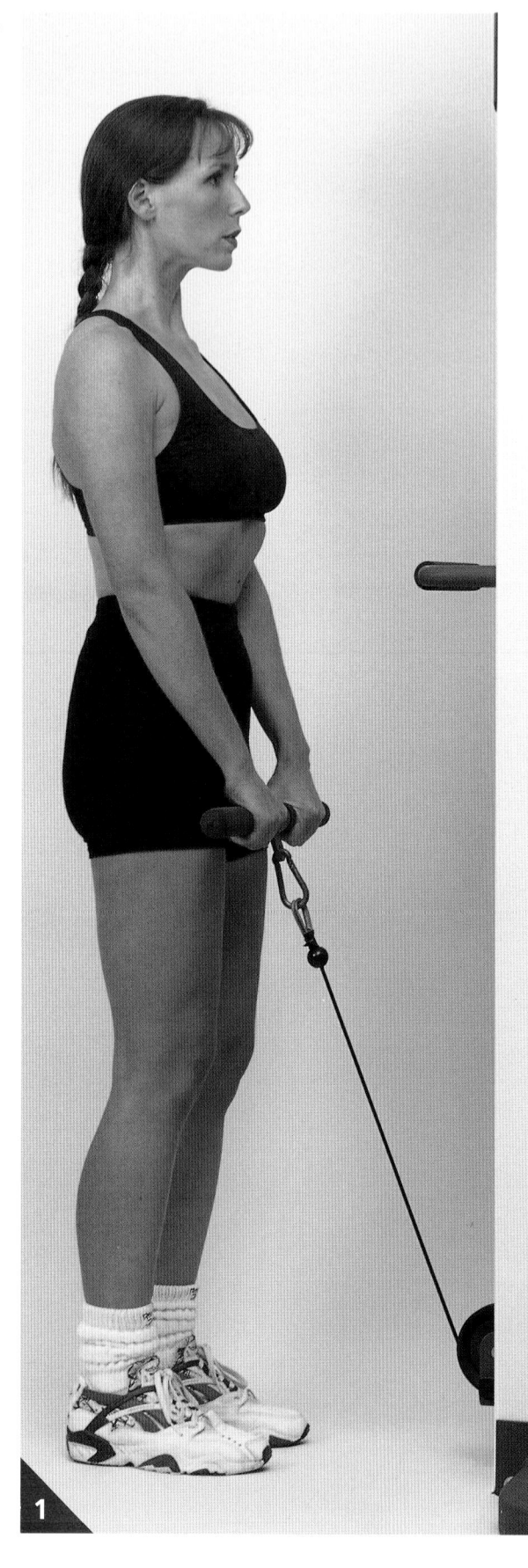

1

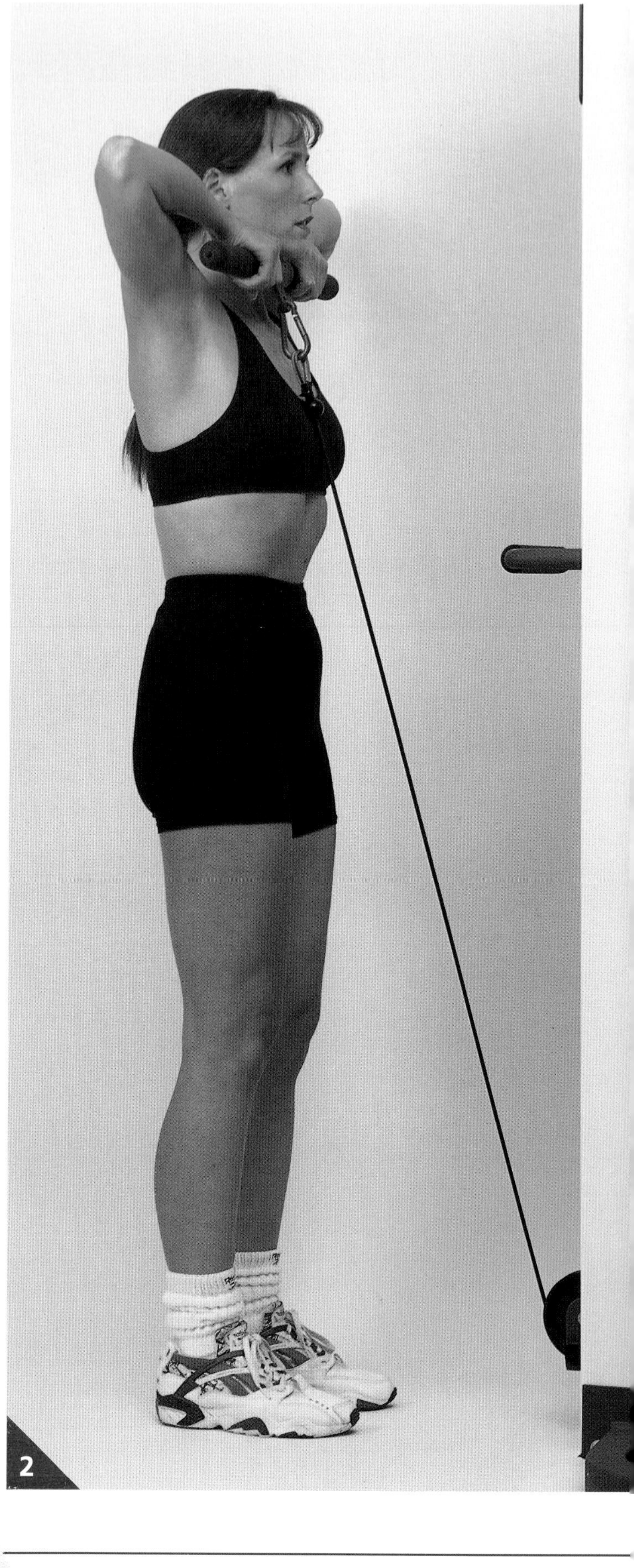

2

UPRIGHT ROW

Upright row

This exercise develops the anterior deltoid and the trapezius muscles. It is usually done with a barbell, but a machine can be used.

With an overhand grip, the hands should be held close together, the bar is raised from the thighs to under the chin, and then lowered slowly. Be careful not to use the lower back when lifting.

1

"The hands should be held close together, and lowered slowly. Do not use the lower back when lifting."

2

1

The Clean

This exercise is a great compound exercise, working the shoulders, back, legs, arms, and gluteus. The feet are one shoulder-width apart and the knees are soft. Hold the bar in an overhand grip, slightly wider than the shoulders. The weight is lifted off the floor and the bar is rolled up from the elbows to shoulder height. This position is held with the elbows tucked into the side of the body. Next, lower the bar to the floor in two controlled moves, first by extending arms to thighs, secondly, by lowering the bar to the floor.

2

REMEMBER

This exercise is difficult.
Ensure you

■

Bend your knees
when picking up the
weight

■

Keep your back straight

■

Keep your knee
alignment
over your toes

■

Don't swing your back
when lifting the bar to
your chest.

3

DUMBBELL ALTERNATE SHOULDER RAISE

Dumbbell alternate shoulder raise

Designed to develop the anterior deltoid, here the dumbbell is held in an overhand grip and movement starts from the thigh. Keeping the arm straight and elbow soft, it is raised to shoulder height then lowered to the thighs. Each arm is used alternately because this can help with balance and control.

1

2

> "*The dumbbell is held in an overhand grip and movement starts from the thigh. Help balance and control by using each arm alternately.*"

SHOULDER SHRUG

Shoulder shrug

This exercise develops the trapezius muscles and deltoids. Using dumbbells, the weights are held beside the thighs. The movement involves raising the shoulders toward the ears, then back down again. You can vary this by rolling the shoulders forward or backward, bringing the upper back and shoulders into the movement respectively.

WORKOUT ROUTINE

Basic shoulder workout
Military press
3 sets x 10 reps
Cable lateral raise
3 sets x 10 reps
Upright row
3 sets x 10 reps

Strength workout
The Clean
4 sets x 10 x 8 x 6 x 2 reps
Military press
4 sets x 10 x 8 x 6 x 2 reps
Cable lateral raise
4 sets x 10 x 8 x 6 x 2 reps
Upright row
4 sets x 10 x 8 x 6 x 2 reps

Endurance workout
Military press
4–5 sets x 14–16 reps
Cable lateral raise
4–5 sets x 14–16 reps
Upright row
4–5 sets x 14–16 reps
Shoulder shrugs
4–5 sets x 14–16 reps

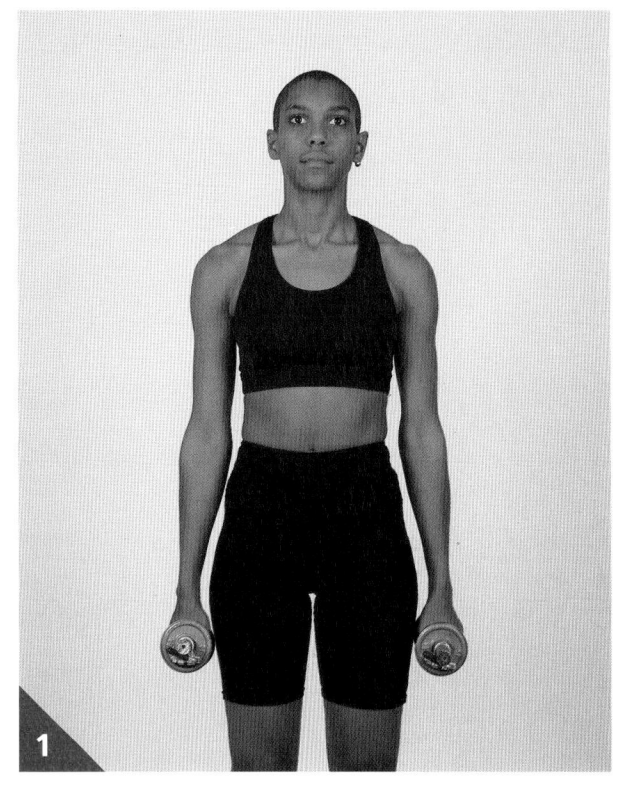

EXERCISES FOR THE CHEST

The chest and bust can be improved greatly through weight-training. Although breasts comprise fatty tissue, which cannot be shaped and formed, the use of weights can strengthen support by toning the muscles across

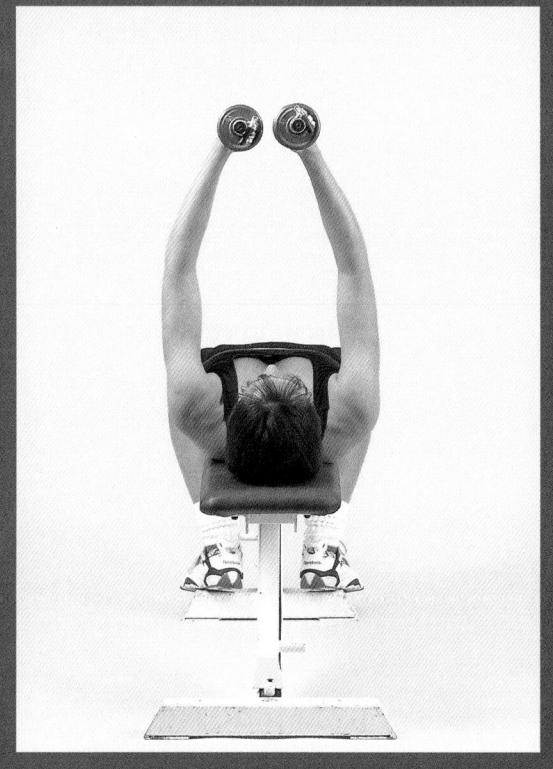

the chest, namely the pectoralis major muscle. The pectoral muscles are very powerful muscles and capable of doing a great deal of work, especially making the breasts look firmer and higher as they receive support, so don't be afraid to give them a good workout. This chapter will focus on perfect pectorals exercises that will strengthen and define the chest.

Perfect pectorals

Pectoralis major

This is a fan-shaped muscle, divided into two parts that cover most of the front of the chest. The muscle can be felt working in movements such as rowing and swimming (e.g. breaststroke). It originates from the clavicle, sternum and the cartilage of the second to sixth ribs. Pectoralis major inserts onto the greater tubicle of the humerus. The clavical portion, lying close to the anterior deltoid, acts with it in flexion. The sternal portion of the chest only works with a downward and forward movement of the arm.

Pectoralis minor

This is a smaller muscle, which sits under the pectoralis major and is involved in a number of movements concerning downward rotation. It has an important lifting effect on the rib cage and is important for good posture.

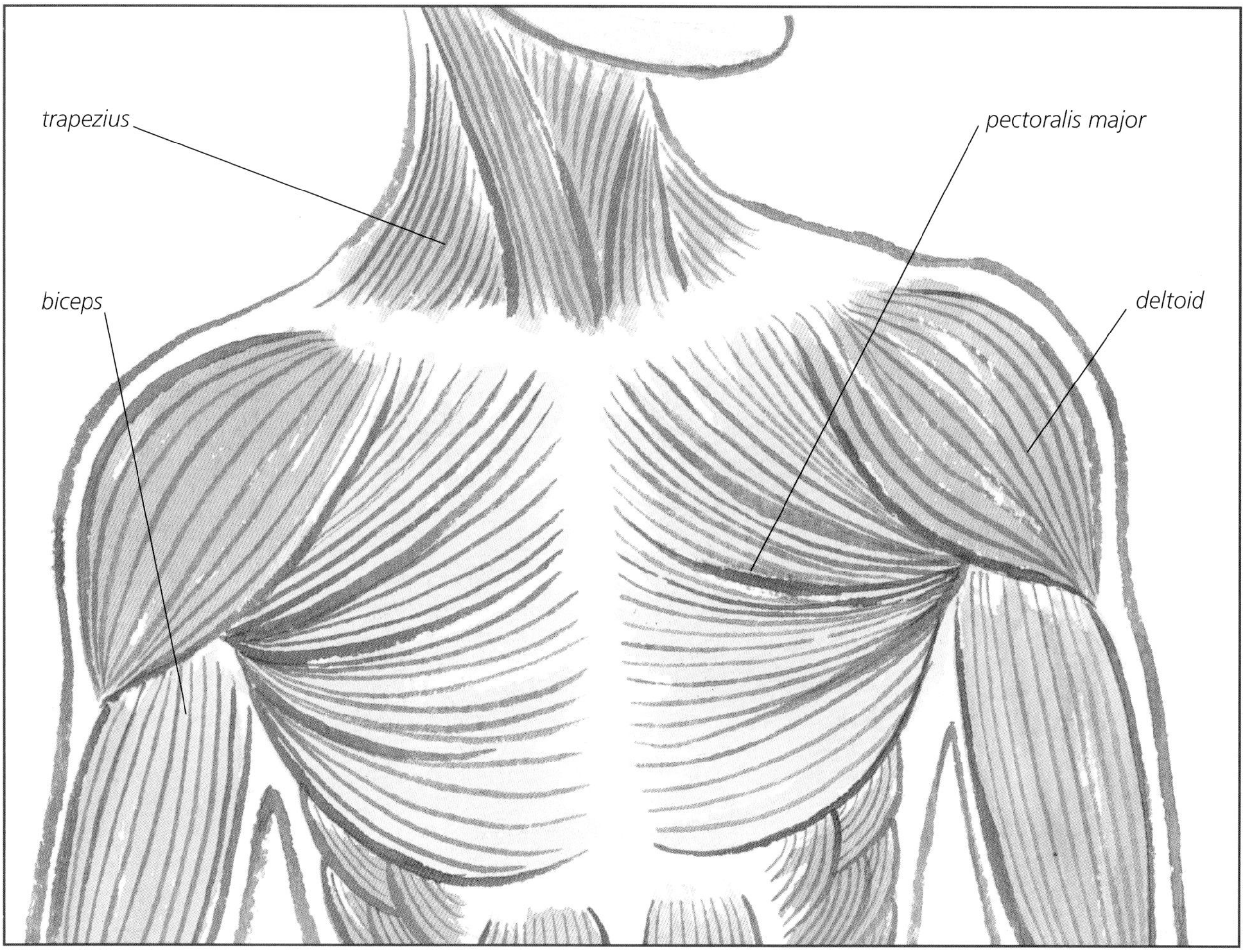

trapezius

pectoralis major

biceps

deltoid

BENCH PRESS

Bench press

The standard exercise for using the pectoral muscles is that of the bench press. It is an excellent exercise for increasing the size of the chest, and strengthening the arms and shoulders. For beginners, an ideal starting position is to place the feet on the bench. This position supports the lower back. More experienced weight lifters will usually keep their feet on the floor for extra support.

The arms should be wide apart and the grip of the bar should be overhand, and the wrist must not be bent. When lying on the bench, your eyes should be looking directly up at the bar. The movement then involves lowering the bar to the chest, then extending the arms to lift the weight.

REMEMBER

■

Do not lift excessive weight without someone to "spot" you

■

Do not "arch" your back when lifting

■

Breathe out as you lift the weight off your chest

INCLINE BENCH PRESS

The bench press can be varied by doing the same action on an **incline bench**. It is particularly beneficial to women as there is greater emphasis on the "upper" part of the pectorals and deltoids. A **decline bench** can also be used and this emphasizes the inferior pectorals.

'Don't be afraid to workout your chest. It is a powerful muscle group capable of working hard.'

DECLINE

DUMBBELLS

1

Dumbbells

These weights may also be used as an alternative to a bar, and the arms can be worked together or alternately. The move is very similar to the bench press – lower the arms to the chest then extend, lifting the weight. This move can also be varied to include an incline or decline bench.

2

DUMBBELL FLY

Dumbbell fly

This is an excellent exercise that works to isolate the pectorals. Lying on a flat bench, the dumbbells are held over the chest, then the arms extended outward toward the floor. The palms must be facing inward and the elbows must be kept slightly bent. This move can also be varied by using an incline or decline bench.

REMEMBER

■

Don't overstretch the chest by taking the arms too wide

■

Feel for the chest extending as the arms move downward

■

Feel for the chest tightening as the arms move upward

■

Breathe out as you lift up

DUMBBELL PULLOVERS

Dumbbell pullovers

A great exercise for developing the chest capacity, this develops not only the upper pectorals, but also expands the rib cage. To start this exercise, it is a good idea to use a flat bench. Holding one dumbbell with both hands, the start position is holding the dumbbell above the head, then lowering behind, slowly coming back up to the start position. The more advanced version of this is to lie across a bench keeping the hips low, with your feet firmly on the floor. The dumbbell should be raised above the chest and then lowered.

Pec Dec

One of the most popular machines in a gym, the Pec Dec develops definition in the pectoral muscles. Check the adjustments so that the seat height is correct for you as arms must be parallel to the floor, and your back supported. Push the arms together. The aim is to squeeze the pectoral muscles. This movement must not be swung nor should the movement start too far back, forcing the shoulders and chest to overstretch.

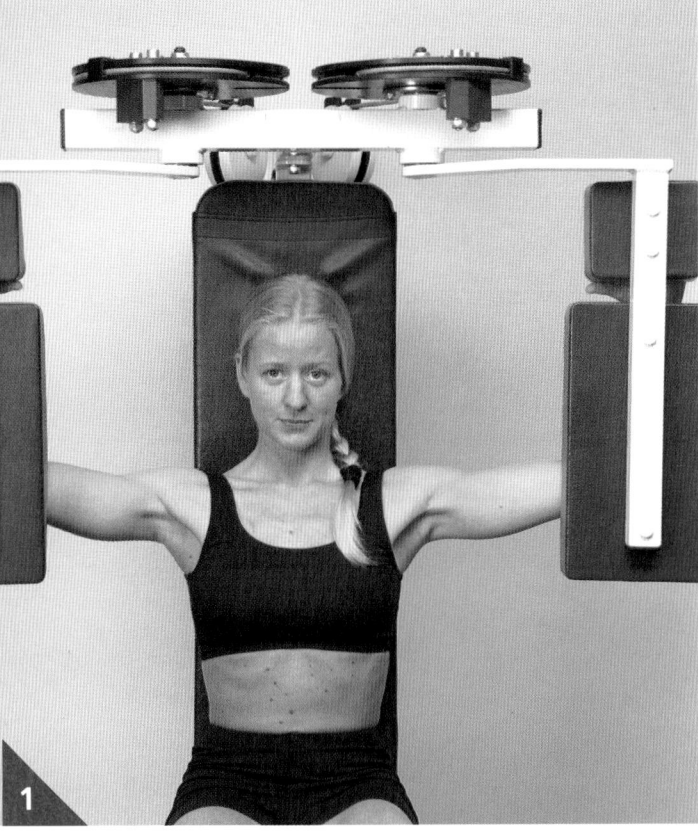

1

PEC DEC

2

WORKOUT ROUTINE

Basic workout
Bench press
3 sets x 10 reps
Dumbbell flys
3 sets x 10 reps
Pec Dec
3 sets x 10 reps

Strength workout
Bench press/incline press
4 sets x 10 x 8 x 6 x 2 reps
Dumbbell press or flys
4 sets x 10 x 8 x 6 x 2 reps
Pec Dec
4 sets x 10 x 8 x 6 x 2 reps
Dumbbell pullovers
4 sets x 10 x 8 x 6 x 2 reps

Endurance workout
Bench press/incline press
4–5 sets x 14–16 reps
Dumbbell flys
4–5 sets x 14–16 reps
Pec Dec
4–5 sets x 14–16 reps
Dumbbell pullovers
4–5 sets x 14–16 reps

ABDOMINAL WORKOUT

N ot many people complain about having abdominal muscles that are too tight. Many people notice when they have gained a few extra inches or pounds, particularly when clothes that used to fit well are now too snug

for comfort. Everybody seems to be in pursuit of lean, well-defined abdominal muscles. They are important in assisting in breathing and in supporting your organs and back, and they play a major part in many everyday movements - bending, reaching, sitting. This chapter will focus on how to achieve toned abs. However, don't fall into the sit-up trap if you are trying to lose inches. Read on . . .

Sit-ups aren't enough

If your goal is to lose weight, then it is very important to combine aerobic activity and healthy eating with muscular strength and endurance. Lying on the floor doing hundreds of sit-ups will improve endurance and strength, but will not give you a flat stomach. Aerobic conditioning will only decrease body fat effectively, and as fat lies in the abdominal region you will need to combine both cardiovascular work with strengthening exercises.

The rectus abdominis is a long, flat muscle originating from the pubis, extending to the rib cage. It is crossed by a series of tendinous bands, which give the abdomen on a well-developed physique that rippled appearance.

Remember, the abdominal muscles are not divided into two parts, i.e. lower and upper abdominals. This erroneous idea is merely reinforced when people state that the abdominal curl (or "crunch" as it is known), isolates the upper abdominals and a reverse curl (lifting the knees into the chest) isolates the lower abdominal region. We can feel a difference in the sections at times because more "motor units" are being applied (motor units being the muscle fibers), however, the whole muscle is active in the movement. Both reverse curls and crunches are effective at working the entire rectus abdominis.

The most effective workout will be performed in a slow and controlled manner, working through a full range of movement. This means more motor units in the muscle are being applied, because the pace is slower, allowing for maximum tension in the muscles. Pulsing or very fast movements involve a very small range of movement, and this is when you are more likely to feel "the burn!" This does not mean that you are getting added improvement in the shape of your muscle or losing fat. The burning sensation is a sign of muscle fatigue. If this happens, you should rest, then continue at a controlled pace. Remember, simply experiencing a burning sensation does not mean you are moving body fat in a given area.

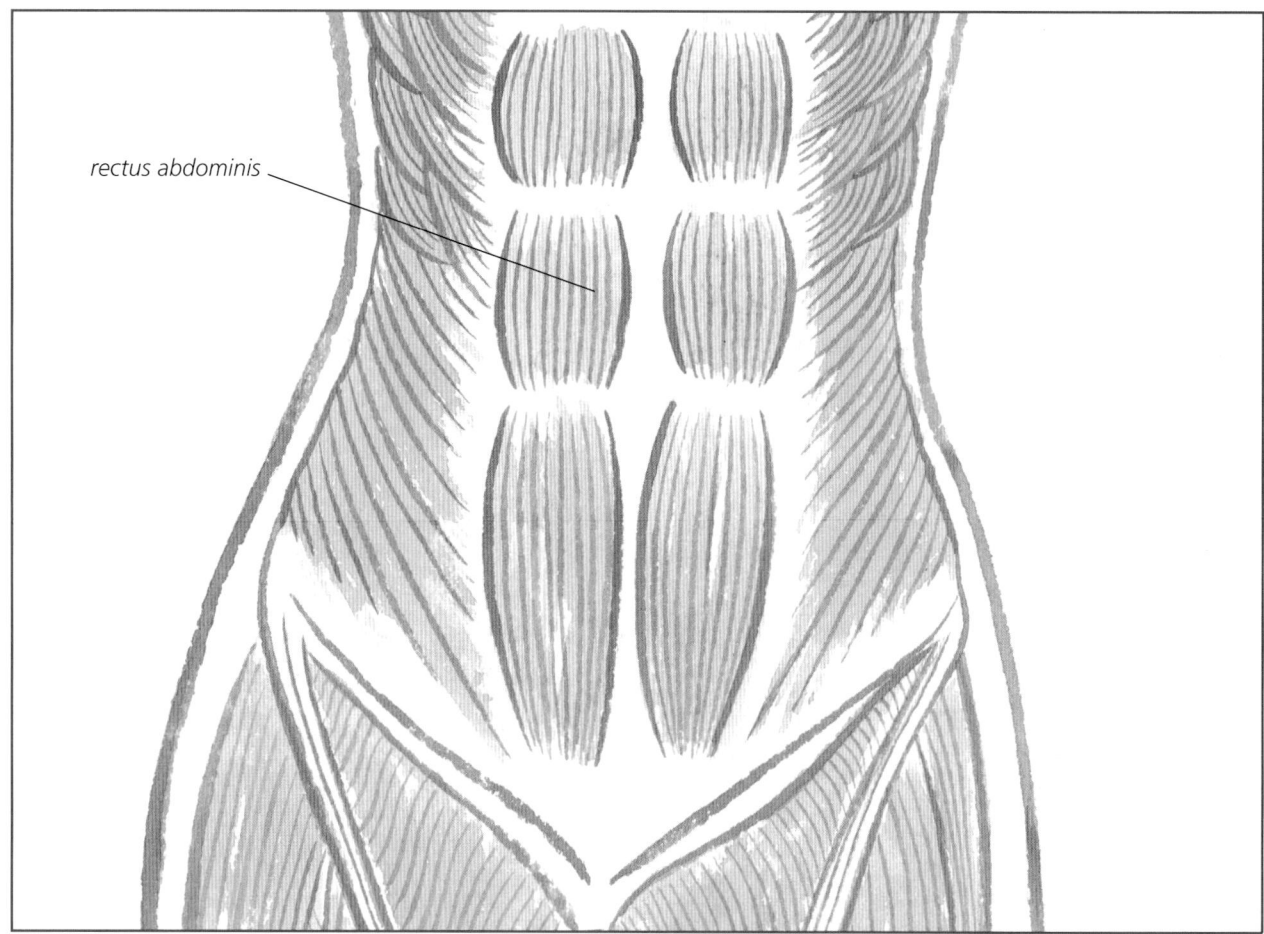

rectus abdominis

Posture is important during abdominal workouts, because neck soreness is a common occurrence in abdominal exercise. The reason is usually quite simple – the soreness occurs due to moving the head too much, causing muscle fatigue in the neck muscles. Soreness usually occurs from having either the head tucked or rolled. This should be avoided at all times! To begin and maintain a crunch (or curl), the head and neck alignment must be in a balanced static, and neutral position. To check, you should be able to fit a closed fist between your collar bone and chin. You should be looking toward the ceiling.

It is **not** recommended that you clasp your hands behind your head. This can cause the head to be pulled forward, placing stress on the neck. Instead, the hands can be webbed, with fingers interlocking and placed behind the head, or gently hold the head and neck with one or both hands. (This does, however, require good flexibility in the shoulders and upper back, which will be achieved by strengthening the muscles in this area.)

REMEMBER

■

Maintain or support your neck in line with the spine

■

Avoid letting your neck roll forward, having the chin resting on the chest, or lifting the chin toward the ceiling

■

Do not fling your head around

■

Minimize arm movements

■

Do not use weights if you get any pain whatsoever

■

Concentrate on lifting up from chest with relaxed shoulders

ABDOMINAL CRUNCH

Abdominal crunch

This is the core exercise for abdominis. It works the rectus abdominis along with help from the external and internal oblique muscles. You should lie on your back (known as the supine position), with heels on the floor close to the buttocks. Arms can be in a variety of positions, but must never be thrown around! All the emphasis should stay in the abdominal region. Keep the head and shoulders relaxed. The neck should not be flexed, e.g. chin resting on the chest, as this makes breathing difficult. It also causes the muscles in the neck to fatigue, causing pain. Moving the head will also tire the neck, causing pain.

Variations to the crunch

There are numerous arm movements that can be used in crunches. All of them use the whole abdominal region, e.g.:

1 Lifting the arms to the ceiling, then down to the chest
2 Alternating each arm to the opposite knee
3 One foot resting on the knee and raising the opposite elbow to the knee
4 Some gyms may have a crunch machine which can add variety to an abdominal workout

'Relax your upper body. If you can smile - it's a good sign. Remember, the effort comes from your abdominal region.'

REVERSE ABDOMINAL CURL

Oblique crunch

This involves rolling bent knees to one side (don't force the legs to the floor), then lift up. The external obliques on that side, and the internal oblique on the opposite side become the prime movers.

Reverse abdominal curl

This involves the same starting position as the crunch but instead of lifting the shoulders from the floor, which involves spinal flexion, the knees are lifted and pulled toward the chest. The range of movement is more limited than the crunch, but it does avoid the neck and shoulder pain that some people feel when performing crunches. Remember that the knees must come up toward the chest and the legs should not fling up toward the ceiling.

WORKOUT ROUTINE

This routine will vary from person to person. The following may be difficult for beginners, yet too easy for advanced trainers. It is only intended as a guide. You may like to do five sets of 20, or three sets of 50 repetitions. Whatever your level of strength or stamina, always keep good form and increase the intensity or duration of your abdominal workouts when they become too easy!

You can increase the intensity by lifting up on two counts and coming down in one count; or lifting for three counts and lowering in two counts.

Crunches
3 sets x 20 reps
Oblique crunches
3 sets x 20 reps
Reverse abdominal curls
3 sets x 20 reps
Reverse abdominal curls with pelvic lift
3 sets x 20 reps

Reverse abdominal curl with pelvic lift

Here the legs are raised toward the ceiling, then the knees are brought down toward the chest, lifting the pelvis slightly off the floor. Be careful not to lift the lower back off the floor as this may cause lower back pain. This exercise will be difficult to perform if you have weak hamstring and lower back muscles.

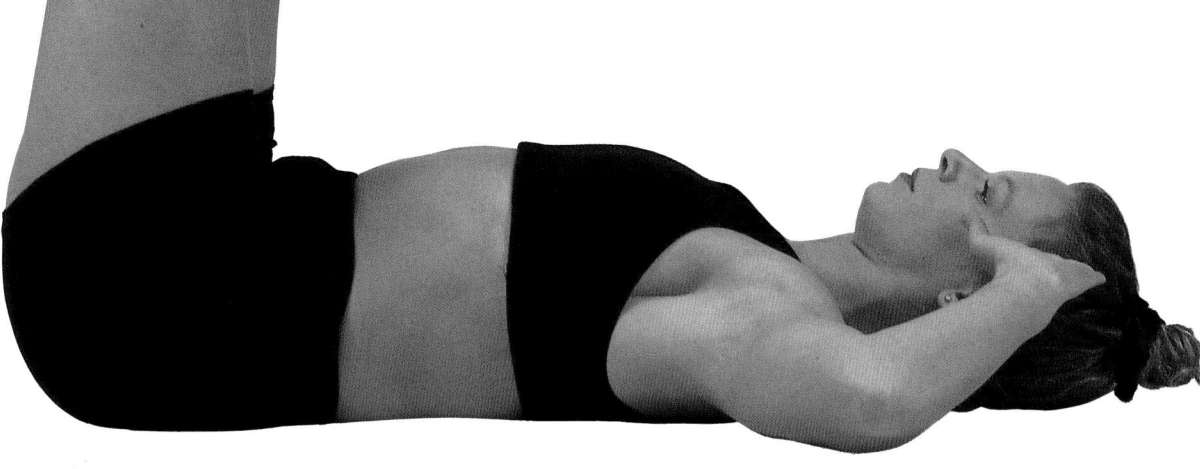

EXERCISES FOR THE BACK

A shapely back enhances the alignment of the body, making the waistline appear smaller and sensual. More important, training the back will strengthen it, and help to prevent small or recurring back injuries. Nothing is worse than a "bad back" that can hamper daily activities, and detract from your general enjoyment of life. Adding a few exercises to

your program can help avoid the back pain that seems to afflict the majority of adults.

For women in particular, strong back muscles will help during pregnancy. The exercises in this chapter are aimed at strengthening and toning the back.

B ack muscles are the opposing muscle group of the chest and play a vital role in maintaining correct posture.

The back muscles

Providing a framework for the powerful upper back muscles are the rib cage, the scapulae (the two flat triangular bones in the shoulders), and the shoulder joint. The latissimus, (commonly called "lats"), is responsible for adduction (downward movement) and rotation of the humerus (upper arm). The rhomboids are also responsible for downward rotation and adduction of the scapular and are extremely important for supporting the neck.

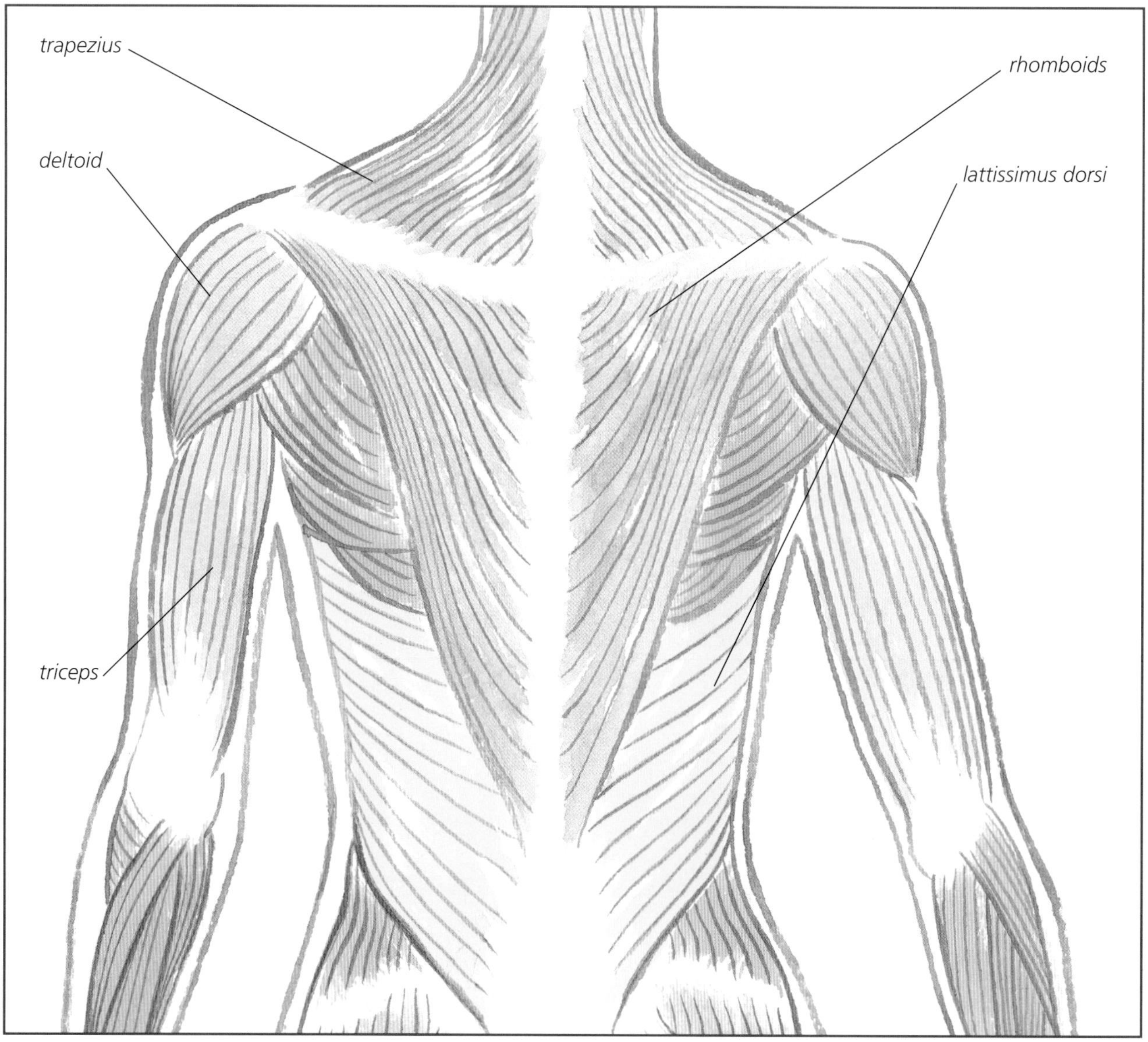

trapezius

rhomboids

deltoid

lattissimus dorsi

triceps

CHIN-UPS

1

2

Wide grip chin-up

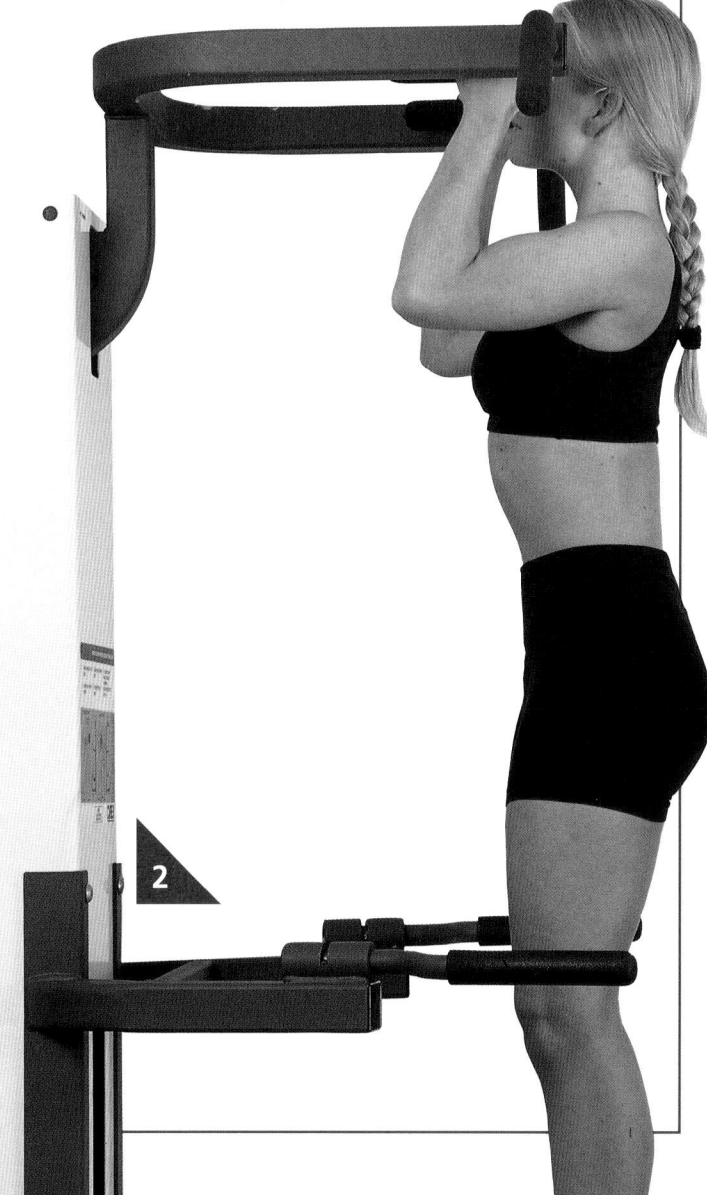

Narrow grip chin-up

Chin-ups

This exercise develops the upper back, trapezius, and arms, and is an excellent strengthening exercise. However, it is difficult. The standard chin-up involves lifting your body weight. While this is an extremely tough exercise, try half a chin-up and gradually build up from there. These moves are very rewarding when done properly.

Use a bench or small box to help you grip the bar properly. Your hands should be slightly wider apart than your shoulders; legs can be crossed so they don't swing. Pull yourself up in line with the bar so that your head is in front of the bar. A slightly easier way to start chin-ups is to use a narrow grip and lifting up toward the chest.

2

LAT PULL-DOWN

1

Lat pull-down

An alternative to chin-ups, this exercise is usually done on a cable machine. Using a wide grip, the bar is pulled down behind the neck and released slowly. It is important not to lift the buttocks off the seat, and if this occurs, reduce the weight being pulled. This exercise can be varied by using a smaller grip or "V" bar and pulling to the front of the neck, down to the sternum. This will thicken the lower part of the lats.

REMEMBER

■

You should not be pulled up from the bench when you release the bar.

2

Single arm dumbbell row

The latissimus dorsi is used independently, therefore allowing for different strength on either side of the body. One arm can be used for support, using either a bench or chair. The movement involves lifting the dumbbell from the floor up to the back, then lowering again. To enhance this move you can, on the downward move, push the dumbbell away from you so that you feel a further stretch in the lats.

1

SINGLE ARM DUMBBELL ROW

2

Seated cable row

This exercise develops thickness in the lats. Using a cable pulley machine, the legs are extended and the knees should be slightly bent. The movement involves gripping a narrow bar or a triangular-shaped bar and, leaning forward from the pelvis, the weight is pulled in toward the abdomen. The back should be kept very straight and the shoulders held back. On leaning forward, this stretches the muscles in the back and you may feel a slight stretch in the hamstring muscles. **Do not** roll your shoulders or back.

SEATED CABLE ROW

2

DEAD LIFT

Dead lift

The following exercise is for advanced workouts and people with good lower back strength.

Dead lifts are a great exercise for the lower back. The feet are positioned shoulder-width apart. The bar can be gripped overhand, but as your load increases, an alternative grip will give better balance and support of the bar. Bend the knees to grip the bar, then rise to a standing position using the legs and back keeping the knees soft at all times. Using the back, lower the weight to the floor.

WORKOUT ROUTINE

Basic workout
Lat pull-downs (machine)
3 sets x 10 reps
Seated cable row (machine)
3 sets x 10 reps
Single arm dumbbell row
3 sets x 10 reps

Power workout
Chin-ups
4 sets x 10 x 8 x 6 x 2 reps
Dead lifts
4 sets x 10 x 8 x 6 x 2 reps
Lat pull-downs
4 sets x 10 x 8 x 6 x 2 reps
Single arm dumbbell row
4 sets x 10 x 8 x 6 x 2 reps

Endurance workout
Chin-ups
4 sets x 14–16 reps
Single arm dumbbell row
4 sets x 14–16 reps
Lat pull-downs
4 sets x 14–16 reps
Seated cable row
4 sets x 14–16 reps

WORKING-OUT THE LEGS AND BUTTOCKS

. . . .

"I don't want big legs" is commonly uttered by women embarking on any sort of fitness program. Training with weights **will not** give you big legs! Fat will make your legs and buttocks big. If you want to embark on a bodybuilding program, then legs

form a huge part of the workout focus. The successful pursuit of toned, shapely legs and a tight butt can be achieved by everyone. The legs are naturally tapered and weight-training is one of the best ways to enhance this. Firm, strong legs are vital for well-being and can be achieved in a short time. Don't be afraid to train your legs.

. . . .

Thighs – quadriceps

There are four muscles which make up the quadriceps. These are rectus femoris, vastus lateralis, intermedius and medialis. They are responsible for extending the leg and flexing the thigh. These muscles are used to straighten a bent knee and work the most when you are sitting and when you stand up. The sartorius is an important muscle, which helps you cross your legs! The longest muscle in the body, it is responsible for flexing, extending and laterally rotating the leg. Finally, the tensor fasciae latae is responsible for flexing and abducting the thigh.

Squats

Squats are a standard exercise for the quadriceps, gluteus, and hamstrings. They tone and strengthen the thighs. This exercise can be performed on what is called a "Smith machine", in which a bar is placed on a rack where it moves freely up and down. The most common way to do squats is by bar alone, placed on a squat rack.

The weight of the bar should be centered on the back of the shoulders and the legs should be positioned shoulder-width apart, with the feet parallel to one another. For the correct action, bend the knees to lower your weight, whilst keeping the back straight and firm. The movement involves lowering to a level where the thighs are parallel to the floor. Exceeding this will cause too much strain on ligaments in the knee. The movement is then completed by ascending to an upright position. This movement should be performed smoothly. No bouncing of the knees or lower back should be experienced.

Variations can be made by placing a slightly different emphasis on a particular part of the muscles. For example, rather than balancing weight on the back of the shoulders, by holding the weight on the front of the shoulders, this puts emphasis on the anterior and inferior portions of the thigh. Placing the feet closer together will enable more emphasis to be placed on the other quadriceps, while a wider squat stance will work out the inner thighs.

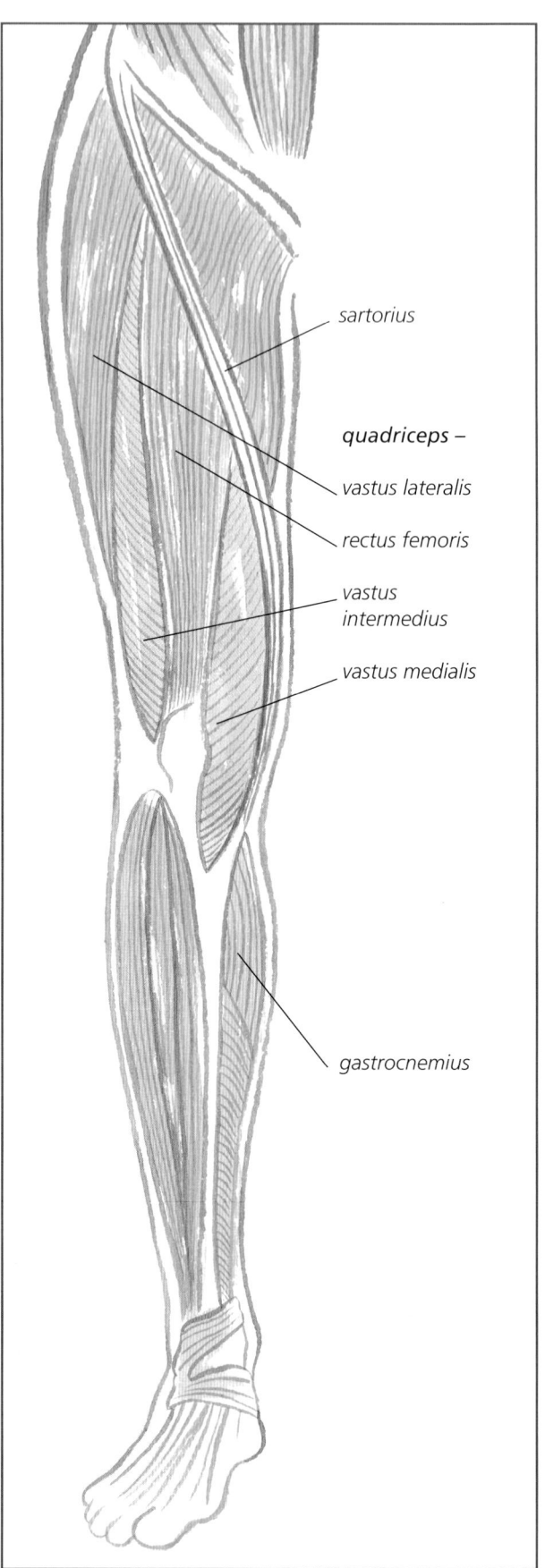

sartorius

quadriceps –

vastus lateralis

rectus femoris

vastus intermedius

vastus medialis

gastrocnemius

SQUATS

1

REMEMBER

■

Hold the head up and keep the back straight.

■

Do not tilt the pelvis forward at the end of one repetition.

■

The knees should be directly over the toe and not be turned in or out during the action.

2

LUNGE

Lunge

This strengthens and develops the quadriceps, hamstrings, and gluteus. This exercise can be performed using either dumbbells or a barbell. For beginners, it is better to start with light dumbbells, and move up to the barbell.

When using dumbbells, the arms should not swing around but be kept firmly to the side of the body. The movement is to step forward with the bending knee almost touching the floor. The beginner should keep the step shorter and not bend too deeply. The more advanced you become, the greater the step and depth can be taken. Add more weight as you progress. As you step forward, the knee must stay just above the toe and should not twist inward or outward.

> *"The lunge is a great exercise for the legs. Try them - they are a challenge."*

Leg extension

This is an excellent exercise to combine with the squat. It isolates the rectus femoris and vastus medialis at the front of the thigh for extra strength and definition. This is performed on a leg extension machine, sitting upright with your back supported. Your feet will be behind a bar and you move your legs from the knee, feeling your quads tighten as you lift. The weight is then lowered to the starting position.

The knees should not be jarred by the upward movement, so be careful not to throw the weights. For additional strength-building, pause for two to three seconds before lowering the legs.

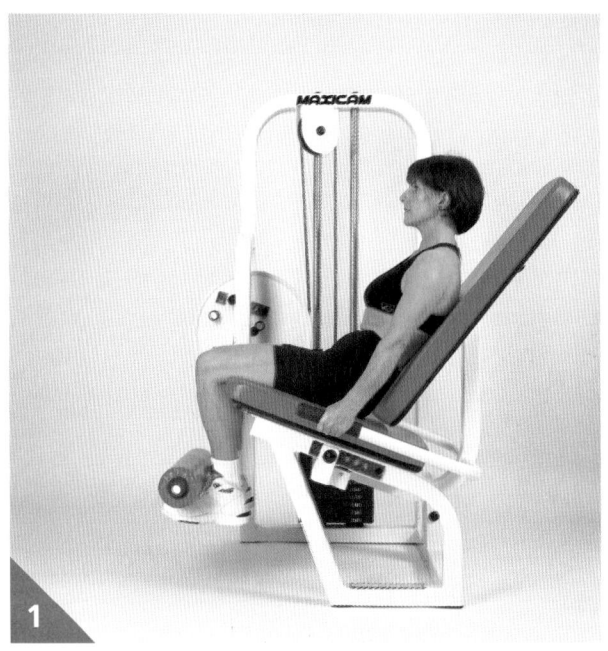

1

2

LEG PRESS

Leg press

An excellent exercise for building strength in the thighs, the leg press also takes some pressure off the lower back. This exercise is performed on a leg press machine and, depending on the type of machine, there may be a variety of angles at which the exercise can be performed.

The starting position requires the legs to be bent at the knee, close to the chest, and then straightened by pushing against the weight. Hands are kept by the side of the body and the back must be supported throughout.

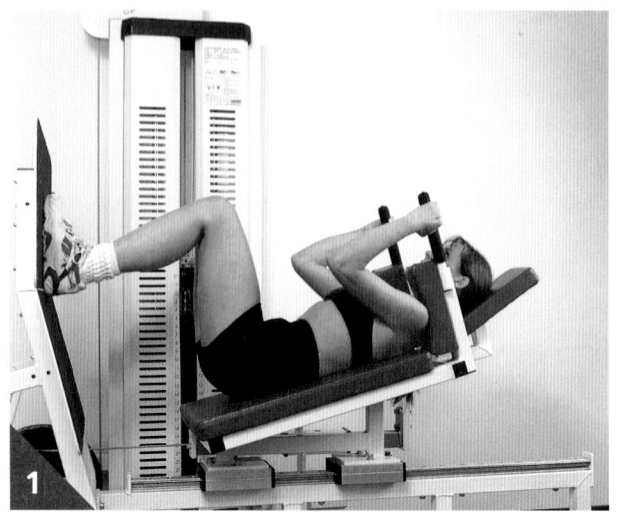

Hamstrings

Once again, there are a large number of muscles in the back of the legs, the most well-known being the hamstrings. These act in unison with the quadriceps to make movement possible. When the quadriceps are being flexed, the hamstrings are extended and vice versa. The hamstring is properly called biceps femoris and is responsible for flexing and extending the leg. The adductor magnus is responsible for adducting, flexing, and laterally rotating and extending the thighs.

LEG CURL

Leg curl

This exercise develops strength in the hamstring, or leg biceps as it is sometimes known. It is performed on a leg curl machine, on which you lie face down on a bench making sure that your knees fit comfortably at the end of the bench. The feet are hooked under a padded mechanism and should rest on the Achilles heel. The lower leg moves upward from the knee in a curling movement toward the buttocks. It is important to keep the hip and back firmly on the bench so as not to arch the back.

The movement should be performed in a controlled and moderate manner. As with the leg extension exercise, you can hold the move at the top of the exercise for two to three seconds before lowering, gaining maximum strength from the exercise.

Vary the leg curl by performing it in a standing position. This enables unilateral isolation of the hamstring. If you don't have this machine in your gym, you can do this exercise with a cable, that provides continuous resistance through the full range of movement.

STANDING HEEL RAISE

STANDING HEEL RAISE

Calf muscles

These muscles are the most prone to soreness if they are not warmed-up and stretched properly. The muscles most significant for working-out are the gastrocnemius and the soleus. The gastrocnemius flexes the foot and the leg, while the soleus is exclusively used for flexing the foot.

Standing heel raise

A standing heel raise is the most commonly performed exercise for this muscle group. In many gyms there will be a heel raise machine to perform these exercises. Where no such machine exists, the feet can be placed shoulder-width apart and the toes are firmly placed on a supported platform, with the heels unsupported. The movement involves raising up onto the toes as far as possible, then lowering as far as possible. It is important that your hips do not move forward, nor should the back be arched.

This exercise can be varied by turning the toes inward or outward. The action can also be performed in a seated position by holding a bar across the thighs and raising the toes from the floor. Some gyms may have a machine on which this can be done.

> *"The successful pursuit of toned, shapely legs and a tight butt can be achieved by everyone."*

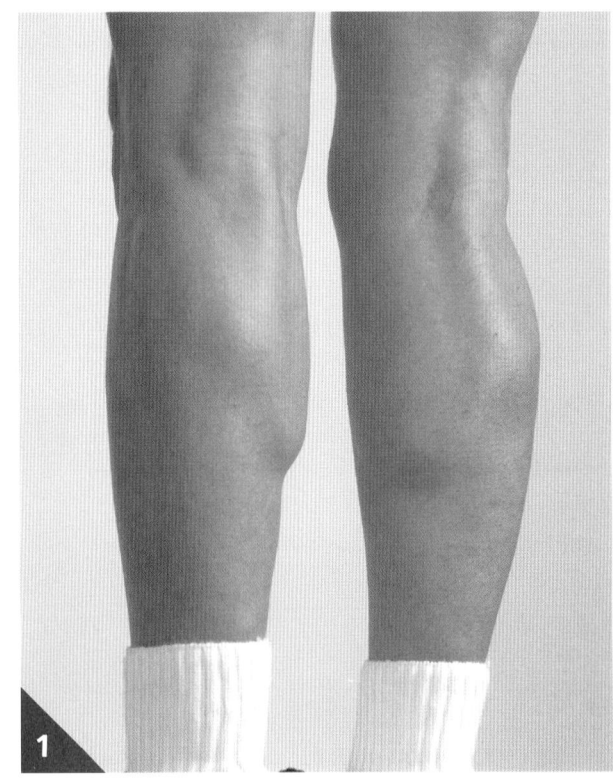

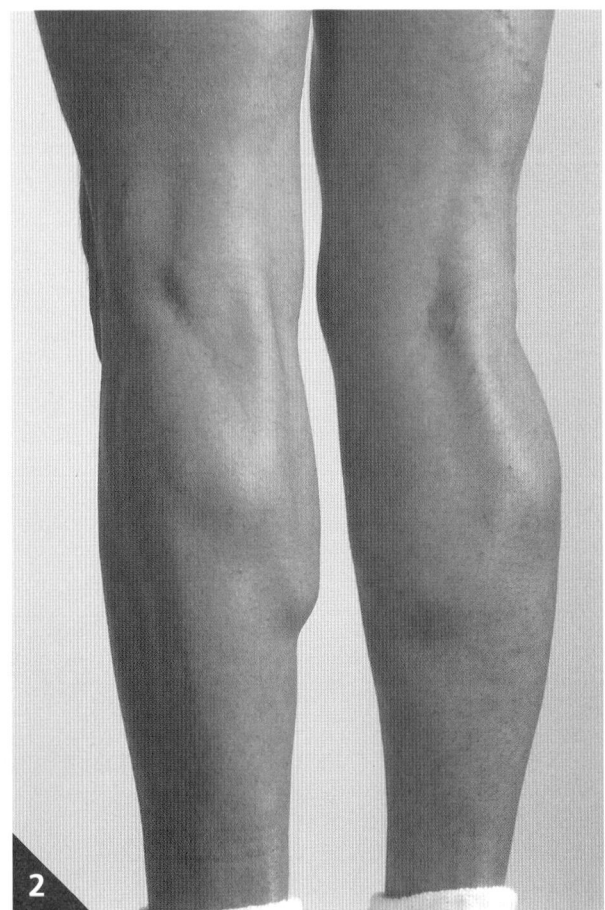

Gluteus (Buttocks)

The legs and gluteus are very closely linked so exercises that use the legs, such as squats and lunges, will also work the gluteus. You need to work the legs and gluteus to get tone into this area. The only way to achieve this is to train legs and hips regularly, maintain a cardiovascular fitness and have a healthy, well-balanced diet.

The two primary muscle groups to work are the gluteus maximus and the gluteus medius. Their job is to rotate and extend the thigh laterally.

The following exercises emphasize the inner thigh:

Cable inner-thigh adduction

This exercise is performed on a pulley machine and works the inside of the thigh. It is a great exercise to finish off a leg workout. Stand with your side next to the pulley machine, with the cable attached to your ankle. The leg is pressed across the body as far as possible, and then released slowly.

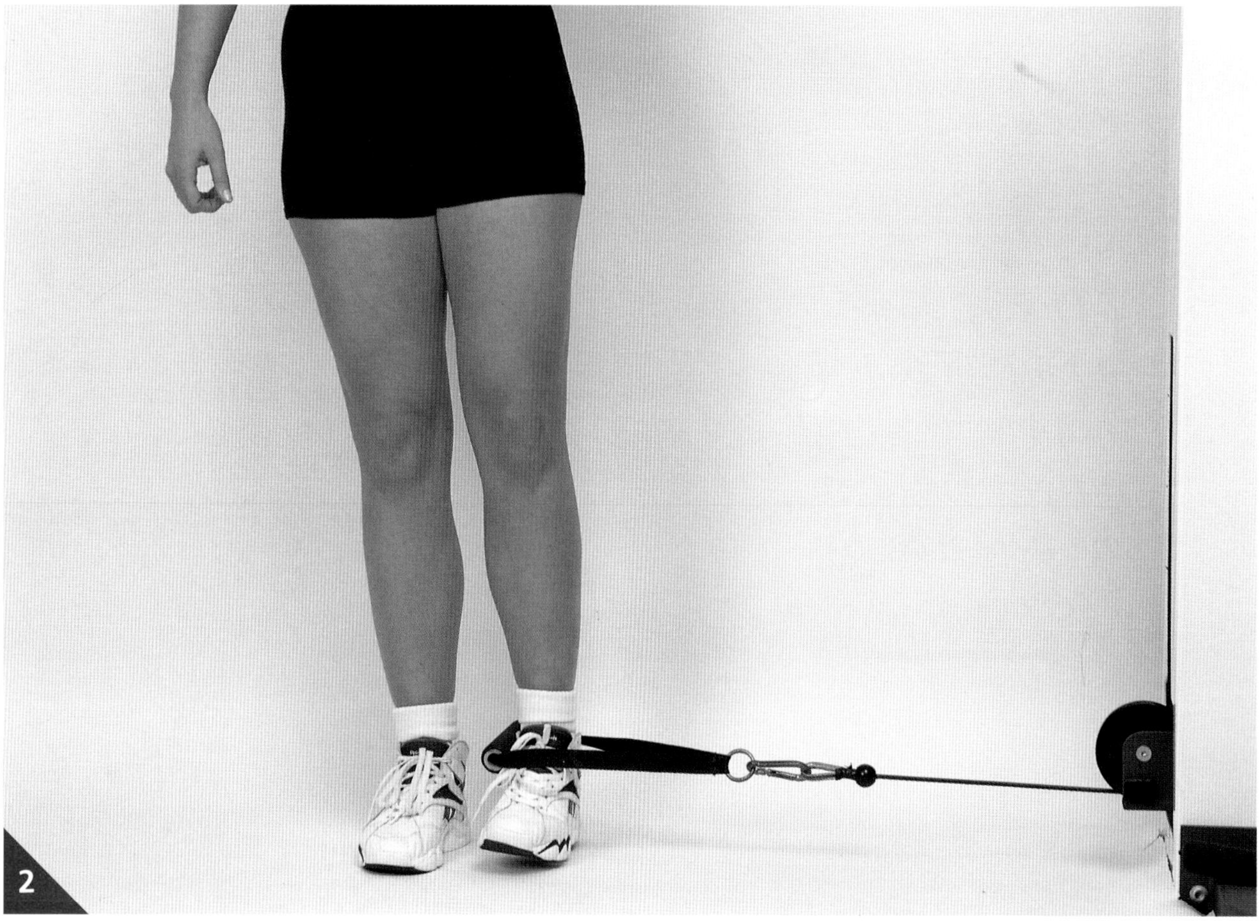

1

2

CABLE INNER-THIGH ADDUCTION

Cable outer-thigh abduction

Similar to the inner-thigh adduction, but strengthening the outside of the thigh in a standing side-on position, the cable is attached to the outside leg (the one furthest away from the machine). The leg muscle is abducted (by pushing away from the body) as far as possible

WORKOUT ROUTINE

Basic workout
Leg extensions
3 sets x 10 reps
Leg curls
3 sets x 10 reps
Standing heel raise
3 sets x 10 reps
Lunges
3 sets x 10 reps

Strength workout
Squats
4 sets x 10 x 8 x 6 x 2 reps
Leg press
4 sets x 10 x 8 x 6 x 2 reps
Leg extensions
4 sets x 10 x 8 x 6 x 2 reps
Leg curls
4 sets x 10 x 8 x 6 x 2 reps
Standing heel raise
4 sets x 10 x 8 x 6 x 2 reps

Endurance workout
Leg press
4–5 sets x 14–16 reps
Leg extensions
4–5 sets x 14–16 reps
Leg curls
4–5 sets x 14–16 reps
Standing heel raise
4–5 sets x 14–16 reps

Vary your training by adding adduction and abduction exercises for the inner and outer thigh.

NUTRITIONAL NEEDS

The saying "you are what you eat" is to a large degree true. However, it is very difficult to go from being a junk-food addict to living on a low-fat, high-fiber diet overnight. By being sensible and constructive, your diet can be a positive and enjoyable experience. Being

obsessive about calorie counting or dreading those weekly "weigh-ins" is not a positive way to live. You have choices, so make positive ones, be in control and make sensible nutritional decisions. Mealtimes should be enjoyed. This chapter is not aimed at telling you what you should or should not eat. Its aim is to provide a guide for how to eat and describes what is healthy for everybody, no matter what their level of fitness.

When it comes to nutritional needs, we usually know the don'ts: no chocolate, chips, burgers, sodas, cakes, ice-cream, and salty snacks and that we should eat more fiber, fruit, and vegetables. The problem today is that fast food answers the demands of hectic lives. Quite often when you are in a hurry, it is easier to grab a chocolate bar rather than have a salad. However, the food you eat is involved in a complex chain of events that provide fuel for the body. The most effective fuel means optimum performance. Food is broken down into nutrients which include proteins, carbohydrate, fats, vitamins, and minerals. Being sensible does not mean being boring: planning meals will save time and, quite often money, in a busy week and prevent the "guilty snack" syndrome.

> *"By being sensible and constructive, your diet can be a positive and enjoyable experience."*

Carbohydrates

Carbohydrates are the principal energy source for the body, providing fuel for the body's work. Ideally they should form about 60% of our diet. However, it is important to distinguish between simple and complex carbohydrates.

Simple carbohydrates are simple molecules that are easily digested. They usually consist of sugars such as sucrose, glucose and fructose, and are sweet to the taste. They include honey, sugar, fruit, vegetables, chocolates, sweets, ice-cream, jams, and cookies.

Complex carbohydrates are more complex in structure and are usually classified as starches. They are broken down into glucose, but this takes significantly longer than breaking down simple carbohydrates due to their complexity. Complex carbohydrates can be found in food products such as bread, pasta, rice, cereal, and potatoes.

Protein

Proteins form the building blocks of the body and are complex chemical molecules. They are built on individual building blocks called amino acids, of which there are 20, eight of these are essential to life. The most common sources of protein can be found in red meat, poultry, fish, milk, cheese, and eggs. If you are a vegetarian, there is an ample source of protein in milk, eggs, and fish. For those who are vegans, a combination of grains, legumes, and nuts can provide the protein required to sustain the body.

The protein question in weight training

Traditionally, it has been believed that athletes, particularly weightlifters, need to consume high amounts of protein. This stems from the belief that more meat will build bigger muscles. This is **not** true: exercise builds up muscle, not extra protein. Therefore, a bodybuilder and marathon runner will have very similar dietary needs – 60–70% carbohydrates and 15–20% protein. Protein is important for the replacement of the body's cells and to restore damaged tissue, which occurs when demands are placed on the body over and above what it is accustomed. Too much protein in the diet will be converted to fat and stored by the body.

Fats

Fat is a vital component of our diet. It is important for the body's maintenance and, when combined with other nutrients, fats form important compounds such as blood lipids, steroids, bile and vitamin D. Stored body fat helps regulate the body temperature, since it insulates the body from rapid heat loss. While fat is a source of energy to the body, it is not the most effective source as it is difficult for the body to break it down quickly into glycogen.

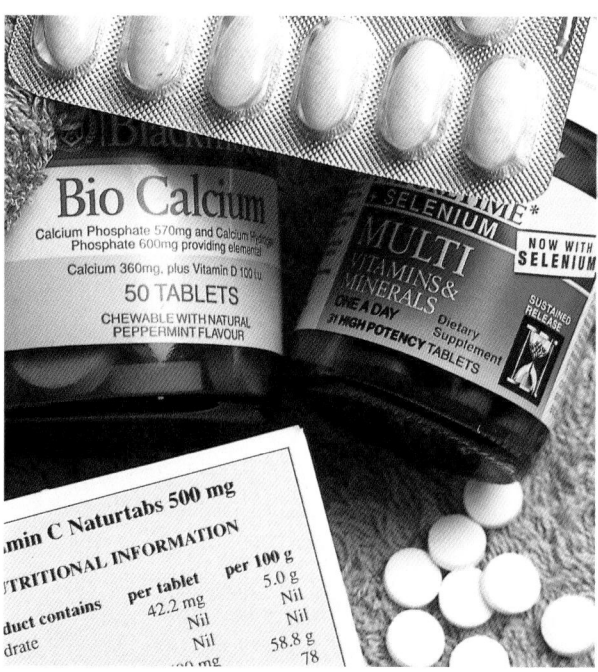

Vitamins

This word, derived from the word *vita*, means essential to life. Vitamins are not usually produced by the body, but are required in minute amounts for body growth, repair, maintenance and development.

Minerals

Minerals are inorganic mineral elements required by the body in the same proportion that vitamins are required – minute amounts. They regulate chemical reactions and body functions. Minerals are also responsible for maintaining and building the body's bone structure.

Water

Our body is made of approximately 70% water. While the body can go for long periods without adequate nutrition, without water the body can die within three to four days. Water is vital for maintaining cell processes and body temperature. Drinking plenty of water is recommended as the body is continually losing water through sweat and elimination. It is important to drink while exercising, because a by-product of exercise is body heat and water loss. Starving yourself of water is dangerous and the effects of serious dehydration can be long-term.

Balancing food intake

There is no doubt that if you want muscle definition you will need to reduce your fat intake. Follow a well-balanced diet consisting of complex carbohydrates and protein. You will be able to enjoy your food, reduce your fat, and have energy for your workouts.

Understanding the nutrients contained in food will enable you to make the right decisions on what is appropriate for your needs. Generally, food is classified in five groups.

Food group	Nutrients
Breads and Cereals	Complex carbohydrates, fiber, and vitamins
Fruit and Vegetables	Simple and complex carbohydrates, vitamins, fat, fiber, and protein
Milk and Cheese Products	Protein, Vitamins A, B, D, and fat
Meat	Protein, Vitamin B, fat, iron
Fats and Oils	Fat, Vitamins A, D and E

Following a good food plan

Eat more:– rice, cereals, pasta, pulses, potatoes
(complex carbohydrates) – fruit, vegetables
– poultry, fish

Reduce:– fats, oils, sugary drinks, alcohol, and sweet
or salty snacks

Do you need supplements?

The selling of vitamins and minerals today is a multi-million dollar business. Many would argue that a well-balanced diet should not require any sort of supplements. The selling point of supplements is that they compensate for poor eating habits and eating "on the run". Poor eating habits affect performance and taking particular supplements will not necessarily replace all the other missing elements of a poor diet.

Cellulite

Cellulite is no more than body fat and the removal of it is the same as the removal of any other body fat. Expensive creams and lotions are not needed – more importantly, they do not work in the long term.

Muscle definition

If you want muscle definition to be visible through the skin, you need, firstly, to build up some muscle, then to reduce your body fat. Starving yourself will not achieve this, but bodybuilders are renowned for severe dieting, particularly in the weeks leading up to a competition. These diets usually involve reducing all proteins, carbohydrates, and even water, to get veins showing through the tissue-thin appearance of the skin. Weighing food and counting the calories becomes one of the most important concerns during these pre-competition periods. Bodybuilders will tell you how exhausted they are from lack of food, so think carefully before you embark on such a program and get proper nutritional advice.

> *"Diet alone will not improve fitness, but a poor diet will certainly affect performance."*

INJURY MANAGEMENT

Feeling pain and soreness can be disheartening. For athletes injury spells disaster; years of training can be frustrated if sudden injury occurs. However, many injuries incurred by weight-training could be avoided if time and care had been

taken to warm-up, stretch, and train properly. Nothing dampens your enthusiasm more than getting pain and muscle soreness.

Injury will limit your goals and training regime. It is vitally important not to overlook injury prevention. The following chapter is to give you some guidance on how to avoid and manage any injury to yourself.

No pain, no gain?

When starting any weight-training program it is vital to start with a light to moderate weight and a small number of sets. Pain and soreness may feel the same, but there is a difference. Muscle soreness is a natural body response when the body has been put through a high level of exertion. Soreness is a natural result of training regimes and muscle soreness can occur between 12–48 hours after exercise. This type of muscle soreness is called **Delayed Onset Muscle Soreness (DOMS)**. The soreness experienced during training is called **Acute Muscle Soreness**, which is usually experienced as a burning sensation. Both of these types of soreness should not be regarded as injury-inducing. Pain, however, is a different matter. It is a bodily response that signals injury or potential injury.

Don't be fooled by the infamous expression, "no pain, no gain." Pain receptors are located within the joints and muscles of the body where they sense damage being done to the body. Listen to pain as it is a warning sign sent by your body to tell you that something destructive could be happening.

"Train sensibly and you will see the gains without the pains."

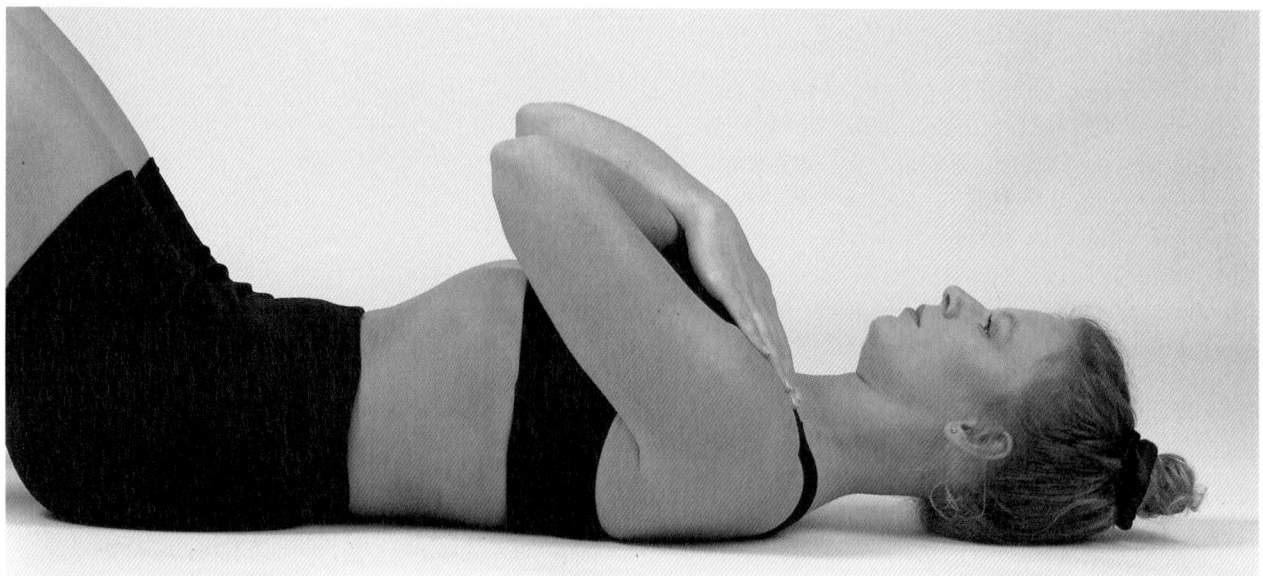

Injuries

The worst types of exercise-induced injuries experienced in the gym are muscle tears (usually caused by lifting weight incorrectly or by lifting weight that is too heavy) and joint injuries. Joints that are particularly vulnerable to injury are the knees, elbow, shoulder, and hip. Muscles, ligaments, and tendons can all be strained or pulled through:

- performing exercises too quickly.
- moving through too great a range of movement.
- lifting heavy weight without an adequate warm-up.
- jerky, uncontrolled movement with weight.

Many injuries can be prevented by following some important and basic steps.

Check equipment
Carefully examine any equipment you use. Dumbbells and barbells must be securely locked to ensure the plates do not slip. Check the weight you use on machines; e.g. if you leave a machine, make sure that when you return to it no one has increased the load between your sets.

If you are using heavy weights, get someone to "spot" you so that should you get tired during a repetition, then a helping hand can lift the weight for you. (Don't be too shy or vain to ask for help and get someone who understands how to "spot" properly.)

Correct posture and technique
Train with the correct posture and good technique to guard against injury.

Train properly
The importance of taking a gradual approach to training cannot be over-emphasized. Get proper rest and do not over-train. Progression, however, must be made in order to enjoy the real benefits of training so don't be afraid to stretch yourself. It is important to take a balanced approach: being over-cautious will make your training routines dull. To prevent injury, you can super-set. For example, split your routines so that you work your upper body one day and your legs the next.

Listen to your body

If you fail to listen to your body's warning signs (such as swelling, soreness, and pain), serious injury can occur. Swelling is easy to detect as the area will be swollen, red, and slightly warmer than the rest of your body. It is a definite sign of injury and should not be left untreated. Soreness can occur through normal training and adequate rest between working a particular muscle group is important for muscle development and repair.

Treating injuries

Many injuries can be self-diagnosed and treated without having to resort to professional help. Such injuries include sprains and strains.

The most common way of treating any injury is the R.I.C.E. method:

R   Rest the injured part of the body and avoid those movements that caused the injury.
I   Ice should be applied to the injured area for approximately 20 minutes.
C   Compression (pressure) should be applied to the injury with the ice.
E   Elevate the injured part to decrease blood flow, which will decrease inflammation of the injury site.

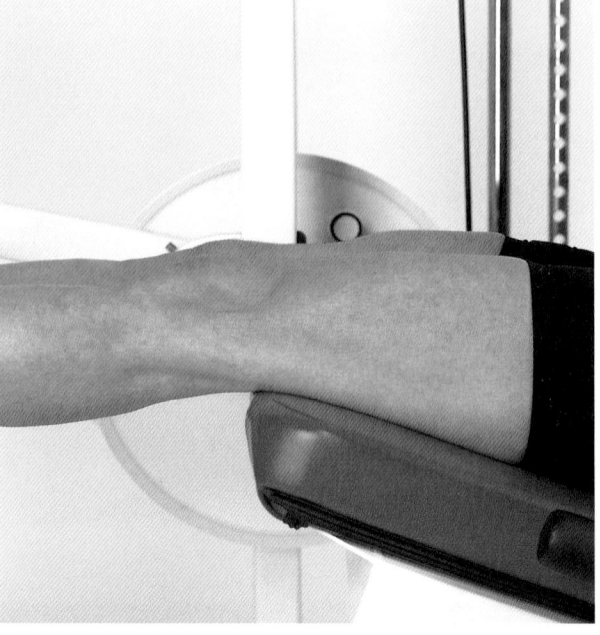

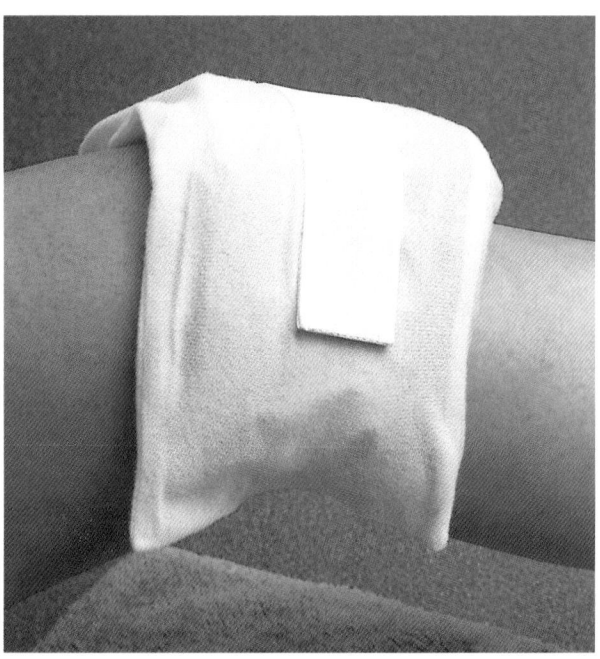

Types of Injury

Injury to muscle

The most common muscle injury is tearing. Pulled muscles are first-degree tears and there is usually localized tenderness. Muscles that tear and cause sudden pain and swelling usually resulting in a loss of muscle use, are known as second-degree muscle tears. Third-degree muscle tears must be surgically repaired.

Injury to tendons

Tendons attach muscle to bone and bear a great deal of stress, particularly when we train. Injury occurs where tendons become strained or inflamed by over-use (tendinitis). The appropriate way to treat such an injury is the R.I.C.E. method. If an injury is not properly treated with adequate rest, tendinitis has a habit of recurring. Once again, proper warm-ups and stretching will reduce the likelihood of such injuries.

Injuries to ligaments

Ligaments connect bone to bone. Injury to a ligament is usually called a sprain. Because ligaments receive a limited, relative blood flow, they are slow to heal. The ligaments most likely to be injured are those in the ankles and the knees. R.I.C.E. is the treatment and professional medical advice should be sought if pain is continuous for more than 36 hours.

SOME HANDY HINTS:

1. Always warm-up properly

2. Stretch prior to and after exercise

3. Don't ignore your body's internal warning signs

4. Don't over-do it if you are a first-time trainer

5. Train with good technique and posture

6. Use the R.I.C.E. method for treating injuries

7. Get medical advice if pain persists

STAYING MOTIVATED

If everyone on the gym's membership list turned up to train, there would be standing room only. So why do so many people have great intentions about getting fit, go to the expense of joining a gym, buy all the gear, but then drop out? All the benefits are well known: weight control, lower blood pressure reduces risk of coronary heart disease, a general

feeling of well-being, and increased confidence and self-esteem and yet, it is easy enough to slip out of the habit of regular exercising. This chapter will provide advice and tips on how to stay motivated, focused, and tuned in to your program.

For many people the greatest excuse for not exercising is limited time. Today we often juggle both family and work commitments, and this balancing act can be very demanding and a tiring experience. There are 24 hours in a day, surely one hour in a day does not seem a lot to ask? Use time constructively by doing something positive for yourself.

Another common reason for not sticking with any exercise program is that it is not fun. Getting fit can be fun if you pick the right program for you and stick with it long enough to see the results. It is important to be realistic about the goals you set for yourself, deciding what you actually want to achieve. Try to be specific – "getting fit" is rather generic. Set goals, for example: "I want to lower my resting pulse rate by 10bpm," "I want to increase the load of weights I use by 10 pounds within two months" and "I want to be able to do 20 full body push-ups."

The key to staying with an exercise program is to follow some simple tips.

Goal setting

Don't just make a New Year's resolution to get strong, fit, and healthy. Set both long-term and short-term goals. If you are really out of shape, give yourself three to four months on basic routines before starting a more demanding program. Plan your daily and weekly routines in advance. Stick to them as much as possible – don't be side-tracked by friends. Remember, without having a clear vision, it is easy to get lost in the fog!

Get over the mental hurdles

People will often give you all sorts of verbal and non-verbal signals that are negative. Therefore, it is important not to fall into the self-doubt traps. Positive thinking leads to a constructive attitude and, with the right attitude, anything is possible.

If someone says you can't do something – do you:
(a) Believe them and don't try?
(b) Believe them, but have a go anyway?
(c) Don't believe them and set out to prove them wrong?

If you want to look a certain way, don't be put off training for that physique. For big muscles, train with a program that will get those results. Seek advice from experienced weight trainers. Avoid those people who are negative about exercise and its benefits.

Exercise as part of your daily routine

Try to make exercise part of your daily or weekly routine. If you train inconsistently, you will never really feel the true benefits that weight-training can offer and you will lose focus on what you are trying to achieve. Join a gym either close to your workplace or near to home. Set aside a particular day and time for training, and do not budge from that training hour, no matter what! Don't make silly excuses, such as it is too cold, wet or hot. (If it is very hot, adapt your training regime to cope with the climate.)

If you are usually too tired to train after work, try training before work or during lunch time. If you prefer to train in the evenings, try to go straight after work. You will be amazed at how all the work worries you had seem to vanish after a good workout. Going home first can often be fatal to good intentions.

If you are busy with small children, try to organize a baby-sitting round, where a group of you can go and exercise together while one of you looks after the children, and then swap. This will reduce baby-sitting costs and everyone will benefit. If your children are at school, do your exercise on the way home from dropping the kids off – and whatever you do – don't look at the kitchen sink!

Increase your pace and challenge your body

Always start your new program slowly and gradually. Don't plan to lift a 50 lb bench press if it is impossible for you to do so. However, set goals to lift heavier weights in three to four months' time or increase the number of repetitions you perform. You may come well under, or over, your goal but it will give you the ability to plan more accurately next time.

Monitor your progress and shape

It is important to keep a record of your training program so that you can see how you are progressing. Most important, do not rely on the bathroom scale. The best way to monitor your progress is a simple tape measure. By measuring your vital statistics, arms, thighs, and calves, you will obtain a more accurate picture of your progress. This should be done every four to six weeks if you are training regularly.

Change your routine regularly

Don't let boredom set in. There are hundreds of ways to challenge your workout and vary your exercise program. Do different sets and combinations. Change the type of exercises you do for particular muscles. Do a power blast workout when you feel stuck.

Keep yourself informed

Read magazines on health- and fitness-related issues. This will keep you up-to-date on any important scientific discoveries on training. Don't rely too heavily on what other people tell you, unless they are expert in their field. Being educated and aware of how your body works will help you distinguish fact from fiction. Reading about a subject is also a great way to stay motivated.

Lifestyle

Your lifestyle can change due to job circumstances, holidays, or pregnancy. Depending on the type of change, fitness can generally be maintained by brisk walking, jogging, aerobics and swimming. Exercises such as push-ups, sit-ups, and a set of adjustable dumbbells can really help when you can't get to the gym.

"Set up a reward regime for yourself. This is a great way to motivate yourself and it is fun."

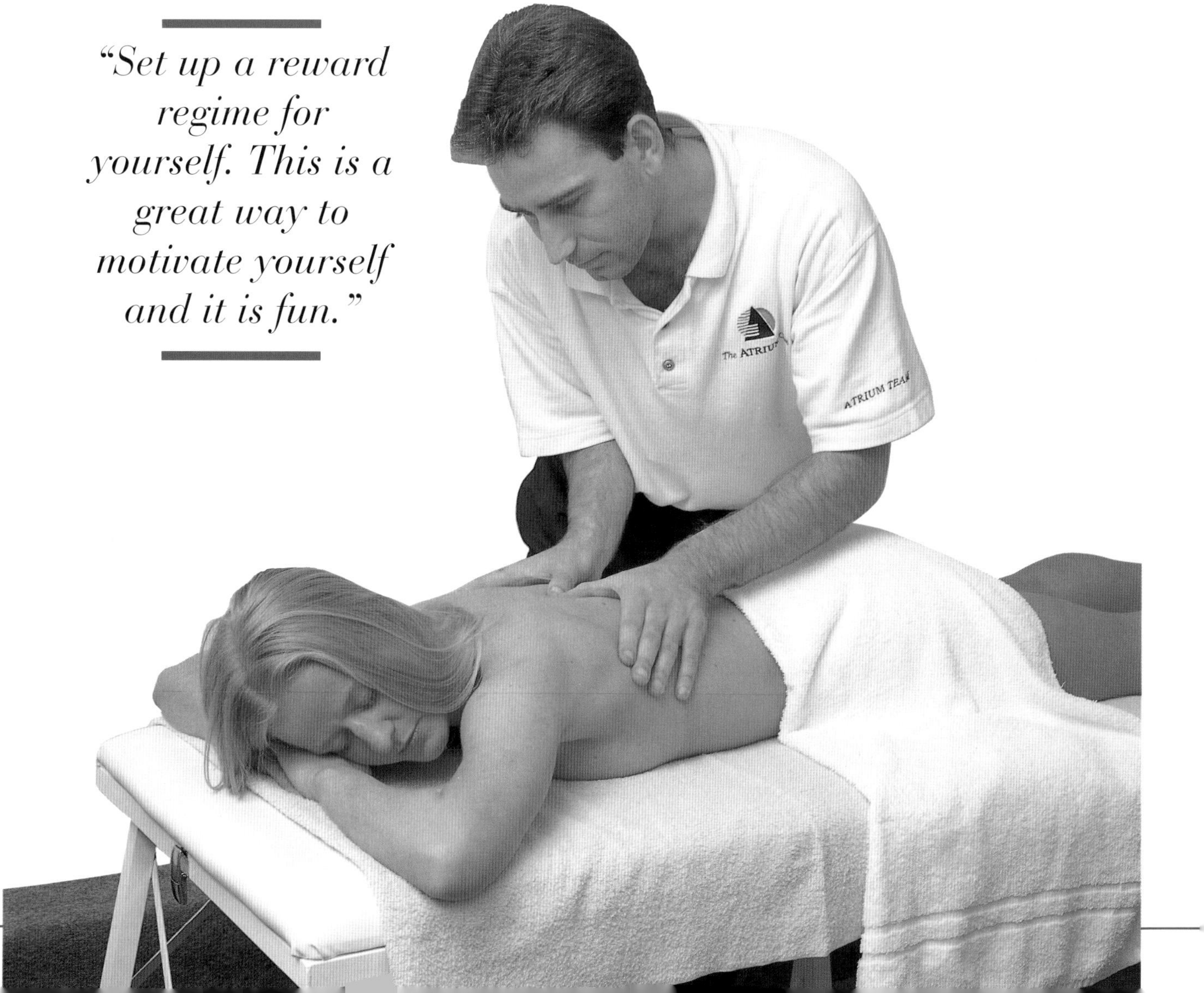

Have a break

Having a break from weight-training should not cause you to feel guilty or worry about muscle turning to fat. If you do stop training, examine the reasons why. Most important, weight-training should be done because you enjoy it, not because you feel pressured to look a particular way.

Don't train if you are unwell. Proper rest is the best way to a quick recovery. If you get very ill, be prepared to train lightly when you do resume training. Getting over a long-term illness puts a lot of stress on the body, so don't try anything too strenuous. A relapse will not be good for your health or motivation.

Rewards

Set up a reward regime for yourself. This is a great way to motivate yourself and it is fun. For example:

- Have a massage at the end of a month when you have really trained hard.
- Purchase some new training gear when you "measure-up" well.
- Have a nice meal with a friend.
- Book a facial or beauty treatment that you've never tried before.

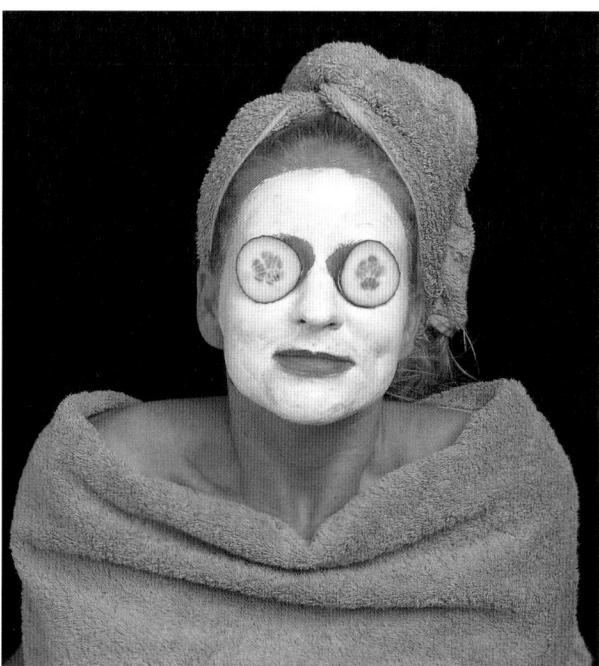

Traveling

If you have a job that involves traveling that means you cannot train as regularly as you would like, do not give up. if you stay at hotels, try to find hotels with a gym. If there is no hotel gym, prepare a condensed fitness regime for yourself while away or on the road. Take a jump rope, some elastic resistance bands or tubing, and, if possible, some dumbbells! Set up a small, simple circuit for yourself along the following lines:

Warm-up with a slow round of jumping rope
5 minutes
Stretch quads, hamstrings, calves, chest, and shoulders *5 minutes*

Circuit
1. Push-ups
   20 reps of full body push-ups (if possible)
2. Abdominal Crunches
   30 reps
3. Jumping
   10 minutes
4. Triceps Dips
   20 reps
5. Squats
   30 reps

If you have some resistance tubing or bands, then you can add exercises such as biceps curls or a lateral shoulder raise to this circuit. Use the exercises in this book and be imaginative! Do not rest too long between each exercise. **Repeat** this circuit three to five times, then cool down and stretch.

Make exercise such an integral part of your life, that to stop exercising would be like leaving home without having brushed your teeth.

PREGNANCY

Pregnancy is a time of great change, not only to your body, but it is also a very personal and emotional time. One of the strongest arguments against women participating in sports has been that there would be likely damage to their

reproductive system, particularly with sports that involve any type of endurance work. If you are a serious exerciser and train regularly with weights, then exercise and strenuous activity can usually be continued throughout pregnancy with safety. But no woman's pregnancy is the same as another so be aware of your own body and respond to its needs.

What should you do on discovering you are pregnant?

Firstly, you need to discuss your level of fitness with your doctor or midwife. If you are already an experienced exerciser, training need only be modified and changed when you change in physical size. However, if there are complications with your pregnancy, then you probably need to re-evaluate your exercise program and take advice from the professionals caring for you.

In many cases, women are encouraged to maintain the fitness program they had prior to pregnancy, as the foetus is well-protected by the pelvic bone. No harm is usually suffered physically or psychologically from exercising.

However, it is not advised that you start a new training program if you have never exercised prior to your pregnancy. You should discuss any exercise program with your doctor and consult exercise leaders/gym instructors for advice.

Many women find that they suffer from extreme tiredness, so sleep and relax positively. During the final weeks of pregnancy, you may be saying to yourself, "Hey, I can't see my gym shoes, let alone get them on without help – exercise, bah!". Don't get disheartened, try going for long walks, swimming, and doing light weight-training for the upper body.

> *"Keep in mind that good upper body strength will prepare you for all the lifting you will be doing after your baby is born."*

There are some important issues that you do need to consider when combining exercise and pregnancy:

1. Discuss your exercise program with your doctor or midwife, and honestly explain your current level of fitness before you embark on any fitness regime.
2. If you have a fitness program, continue to do the best you can at an appropriate level. Be prepared to make moderations along the way to accommodate changes in your body.
3. Beware of heat injury. Your core body temperature is raised during pregnancy, so do not train in hot environments or at the hottest part of the day (usually between 11 am – 2 pm). Wear cool comfortable clothing.
4. Drink plenty of water.
5. Listen to your body. When you feel tired, rest and don't feel guilty about missing a workout.
6. Eat a light carboyhdrate snack at least one to two hours before exercising.
7. Take longer to warm-up and cool down. This will ensure that your joints are ready for exercise.
8. Do **not** diet. Have a well-balanced diet.

Should you experience any of the following, then you should stop training and see your doctor:

- Blurred vision
- Nausea
- Back, pelvic, or hip pain
- Uterine contractions
- Vaginal bleeding
- Racing heart beat

ACKNOWLEDGMENTS

The Publishers are very grateful for the help and cooperation received from

Samantha Nelson, Sharon Sykes, Theresa Bryden and Sandra Davies who performed the workouts, along with the author, and gave more than generously of their time for the exercise photography.

Ron Bradbury and all the staff at The Atrium Club, Ely, Cambridgeshire, England who allowed us generous and pleasant space in their gymnasium and weights room, and gave invaluable advice during the production of this book. Members of Kelsey Kerridge Sports Hall of Cambridge were also cooperative in allowing access to their weights room.

Picture Credits: © 1995 Comstock, INC. : pages 2, 6, 11, 20, 28, 36, 54, 68, 78, 86, 94, 106, 112, 118, 127 ; Gary S. Chapman, Image Bank: page 126.

INDEX